1st EDITION

Perspectives on Diseases and Disorders

Birth Defects

Jacqueline Langwith
Book Editor

GALE
CENGAGE Learning

Detroit • New York • San Francisco • New Haven, Conn • Waterville, Maine • London

Christine Nasso, *Publisher*
Elizabeth Des Chenes, *Managing Editor*

For more information, contact:
Greenhaven Press
27500 Drake Rd.
Farmington Hills, MI 48331-3535
Or you can visit our Internet site at gale.cengage.com

LIBRARY OF CONGRESS CATALOGING-IN-PUBLICATION DATA

Birth defects / Jacqueline Langwith, book editor.
   p. cm. -- (Perspectives on diseases and disorders)
Includes bibliographical references and index.
ISBN 978-0-7377-4787-4 (hardcover)
1. Abnormalities, Human--Popular works. I. Langwith, Jacqueline.
RG626.B625 2010
618.3'2--dc22
                                                          2009052341

Printed in the United States of America
1 2 3 4 5 6 7 14 13 12 11 10

CONTENTS

FOREWORD

"Medicine, to produce health, has to examine disease."
—Plutarch

Independent research on a health issue is often the first step to complement discussions with a physician. But locating accurate, well-organized, understandable medical information can be a challenge. A simple Internet search on terms such as "cancer" or "diabetes," for example, returns an intimidating number of results. Sifting through the results can be daunting, particularly when some of the information is inconsistent or even contradictory. The Greenhaven Press series Perspectives on Diseases and Disorders offers a solution to the often overwhelming nature of researching diseases and disorders.

From the clinical to the personal, titles in the Perspectives on Diseases and Disorders series provide students and other researchers with authoritative, accessible information in unique anthologies that include basic information about the disease or disorder, controversial aspects of diagnosis and treatment, and first-person accounts of those impacted by the disease. The result is a well-rounded combination of primary and secondary sources that, together, provide the reader with a better understanding of the disease or disorder.

Each volume in Perspectives on Diseases and Disorders explores a particular disease or disorder in detail. Material for each volume is carefully selected from a wide range of sources, including encyclopedias, journals, newspapers, nonfiction books, speeches, government documents, pamphlets, organization newsletters, and position papers. Articles in the first chapter provide an authoritative, up-to-date overview that covers symptoms, causes and effects, treatments, cures, and medical advances. The second chapter presents a substantial number of opposing viewpoints on controversial treatments and other current debates relating to the volume topic. The third chapter offers a variety of personal perspectives on the disease or disorder. Patients, doctors, caregivers, and loved ones represent just some of the voices found in this narrative chapter.

Each Perspectives on Diseases and Disorders volume also includes:

- An **annotated table of contents** that provides a brief summary of each article in the volume.
- An **introduction** specific to the volume topic.
- Full-color **charts and graphs** to illustrate key points, concepts, and theories.
- Full-color **photos** that show aspects of the disease or disorder and enhance textual material.
- **"Fast Facts"** that highlight pertinent additional statistics and surprising points.
- A **glossary** providing users with definitions of important terms.
- A **chronology** of important dates relating to the disease or disorder.
- An annotated list of **organizations to contact** for students and other readers seeking additional information.
- A **bibliography** of additional books and periodicals for further research.
- A detailed **subject index** that allows readers to quickly find the information they need.

Whether a student researching a disorder, a patient recently diagnosed with a disease, or an individual who simply wants to learn more about a particular disease or disorder, a reader who turns to Perspectives on Diseases and Disorders will find a wealth of information in each volume that offers not only basic information, but also vigorous debate from multiple perspectives.

INTRODUCTION

Baby Doe, as he would be called, was born on April 8, 1982, in Bloomington, Indiana. His life lasted only a week. However, he had a profound impact on how the American public, physicians, and the legal system view babies born with birth defects.

Baby Doe had Down syndrome, esophageal atresia, and other congenital problems. Down syndrome is a common chromosomal birth defect. It causes distinctive physical features, a wide range of mental delays—from mild to severe—and certain medical problems. Esophageal atresia is a disorder in which the esophagus does not connect properly to the stomach. Without surgery to correct the problem, babies with the condition cannot receive nourishment.

Soon after Baby Doe was born, the doctor who delivered him advised his parents against correcting the esophageal atresia. The doctor told Baby Doe's parents that he would have only a 50 percent chance of surviving the corrective surgery and that even if surgery were successful, he would be severely retarded and would face a lifetime of medical treatment, disability, and dependency. The doctor advised the parents to let Baby Doe die of his birth defect. The parents accepted this advice and decided not to treat Baby Doe.

Many other doctors at the hospital were outraged at the parents' decision. They wanted to perform surgery on Baby Doe immediately so he could receive nourishment. The hospital's lawyers went to court to try to have Baby Doe declared a neglected child and to have the court order medical treatment. However, the Indiana courts decided that the parents of Baby Doe had the right to decide

On January 9, 1984, U.S. surgeon general C. Everett Koop announced new regulations to protect the rights of newborn handicapped Americans. (**AP Images**)

the fate of their child. The case was appealed to the U.S. Supreme Court, but before the justices could hear the case, Baby Doe died of dehydration and pneumonia on April 15, 1982.

The fate of Baby Doe profoundly affected C. Everett Koop, the surgeon general. Speaking to the Milwaukee Children's Hospital of the Medical College of Wisconsin in 1984, almost two years after Baby Doe's death,

Koop commented on his impact: "Baby Doe was a tiny baby boy with multiple congenital defects, yet that child has figuratively taken America by the shoulders and has given us a good shake. Baby Doe asks us to confess how we really feel about our fellow human beings. Baby Doe prods us into revealing whether we are—or are not—the friends of the helpless, the weak, the hurt, the injured, and the troubled."

President Ronald Reagan was also deeply moved by the plight of Baby Doe. He ordered the drafting of federal regulations to prevent what happened to Baby Doe from happening to other babies born with birth defects. The regulations that were drafted, referred to as the Baby Doe regulations, made it unlawful to withhold treatment to a disabled infant. Signs had to be prominently displayed in obstetrics wards of hospitals providing a telephone hotline to call if anyone was aware of incidents involving the withholding of treatment from a disabled newborn. Doctors' groups and others vehemently opposed the regulations, believing they were intrusive and created an atmosphere of fear. Eventually the regulations were struck down by the U.S. Supreme Court on the grounds that the 1973 law, upon which the regulations were based, did not apply to infants.

A second set of Baby Doe regulations were then ordered by the U.S. Congress under the Child Abuse Amendment Act of 1984. These regulations are still on the books and make it a crime of child abuse to withhold lifesaving treatment from a seriously ill infant. States receiving federal money for child abuse programs must develop procedures to report instances of neglect, defined as the withholding of treatment unless a baby is irreversibly comatose or the treatment is "virtually futile" in terms of the newborn's survival.

Many doctors and ethicists believe the Baby Doe regulations were necessary at the time. However, many feel that the regulations have had some unintended consequences. In December 2005 the President's Council on

Bioethics discussed the Baby Doe regulations. Pediatrics professor Norman Fost explained that in the 1970s it was common for babies born with Down syndrome or other birth defects to have nourishment withheld and to be allowed to die. According to Fost:

> The turning point came in the mid-1980s when President Reagan implemented so-called Baby Doe regulations that prohibited discrimination on the basis of handicap. And to the best of my knowledge, since 1985, there has not been a single case of a child who has—with Down's Syndrome or spina bifida, the other common malformation—who has died due to withholding of standard care simply on the basis of having Down's Syndrome or spina bifida.

Fost goes on to say, however, that there has been a rebound effect from the Baby Doe regulations. According to Fost:

> This long history of undertreatment, . . . what is now widely agreed to be inappropriate withholding of treatment in such children, has been replaced by what many of us consider overtreatment. . . . What we have now is a country in which children receive treatment regardless of whether it serves any interest of theirs, children who have little or no prospects for a meaningful or long life, but suffer in intensive care units or in intensive care units in their homes, in part as a result of fear of legal repercussions, in part due to what I consider misinterpretation of the famous or infamous Baby Doe regulations.

According to neurologist James Bernat, the Baby Doe regulations leave parents and their seriously ill infants to fend for themselves once they are no longer in the hospital. Writing in his 2008 book *Ethical Issues in Neurology,* Bernat says:

Critics of Baby Doe regulations say that the legislation does nothing to help parents financially or emotionally cope with having a severely handicapped newborn. **(Denise Hager/Catchlight Visual Services/Alamy)**

There is a tragic irony to the Baby Doe regulations. Although they mandate aggressive medical treatment for the seriously ill infant, no regulations provide for the continuing care of the infant if it survives to return home. The emotional and financial burden on families caring for these infants is enormous. Some families find caring for a severely disabled infant to be an ennobling experience, but others are destroyed by it.

Author Mark Hunter, in the journal the *American*, wrote about a mother who has been devastated by caring for her severely disabled daughter. In the 1998 essay "The Miracle and the Shame," Hunter writes:

> Diane Maroney of Parker, Colorado, is a former neonatal nurse whose four-year-old daughter, MacKenzie, born at 25 weeks, remains stricken with life-threatening chronic lung disease. Maroney will never forget the bedside words of her daughter's neonatologist as he explained why he'd overruled their tearful decision to abjure aggressive measures: "We are doctors, and we're here to do what doctors do, regardless of whether or not we ourselves have to live with the long-term consequences." Despite her love for her daughter, Maroney says that if she learned her next child were expected to arrive very prematurely, "I would not save her. I don't believe putting them through the pain and suffering is worth it."

Some physicians have called for a rewriting of the Baby Doe regulations. Writing in the March 2005 issue of the journal *Pediatrics*, professor of medical humanities Loretta Kopelman says, "The Baby Doe rules should be challenged by the American Academy of Pediatrics (AAP), because they impede individualized and compassionate care for children advocated by the AAP, and they give too little consideration to parental consent, clinical judgment, and duties to minimize unnecessary suffering and treat others the way we wish to be treated."

A great deal has changed in the medical field and in society's attitudes since the 1980s, when the Baby Doe regulations were drafted. Medical advances have enabled doctors to save the lives of many children who would have died in the past and to improve the lives of children born with birth defects and serious disabilities. Additionally, disabled people have made educational, cultural, and societal strides. Yet for parents, finding out their child has a birth defect can be devastating and scary. Children and adults with birth defects face many profound challenges in their lives. In *Perspectives on Diseases and Disorders: Birth Defects*, the contributing authors discuss the latest medical and scientific knowledge about birth defects, debate controversial issues, and provide insight into what it means to live with a birth defect or to love someone who does.

CHAPTER 1

Understanding Birth Defects

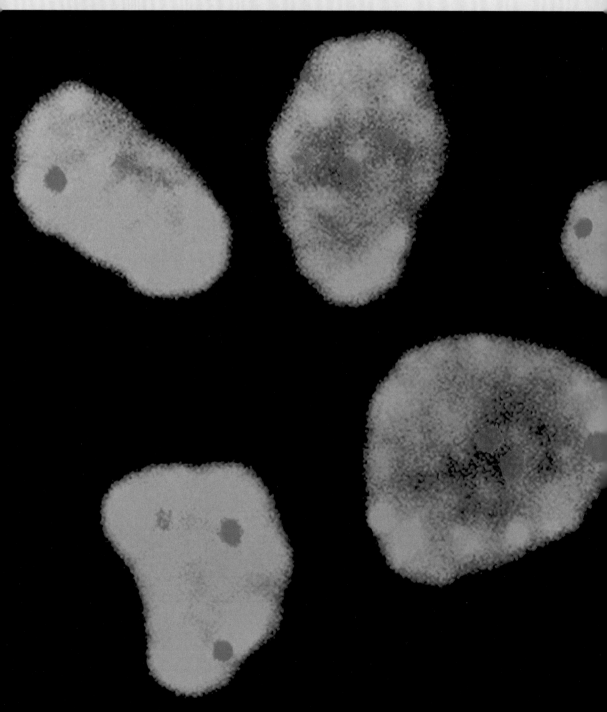

An Overview of Birth Defects

Karen Ericson and Teresa G. Odle

In the following article Karen Ericson and Teresa G. Odle provide an overview of birth defects. According to Ericson and Odle, the specific cause of most birth defects is unknown. However, there are several possible factors such as maternal exposure to teratogens that can increase the risk of birth defects. A teratogen is any substance that can cause malformations of an embryo or fetus and result in a birth defect. Teratogens include alcohol and drugs, chemicals, radiation, viruses, and parasites. Certain genetic factors such as extra or missing chromosomes are also associated with birth defects. In addition to discussing the causes of birth defects, Ericson and Odle provide information about their diagnosis, treatment, and prevention. Ericson is a registered nurse and medical writer. Odle is a nationally recognized medical writer.

Birth defects are physical abnormalities that are present at birth; they also are called congenital abnormalities. More than 3,000 have been identified.

SOURCE: Karen Ericson and Teresa G. Odle, "Birth Defects," *Gale Encyclopedia of Medicine*, 2006. Reproduced by permission of Gale, a part of Cengage Learning.

Photo on facing page. A fluorescence in situ hybridization (FISH) micrograph showing Down syndrome chromosomes (red) in a fetus's cell nuclei (blue). (SPL/Photo Researchers, Inc.)

Birth defects are found in 2–3% of all newborn infants. This rate doubles in the first year, and reaches 10% by age five, as more defects become evident and can be diagnosed. Almost 20% of deaths in newborns are caused by birth defects.

Abnormalities can occur in any major organ or part of the body. Major defects are structural abnormalities that affect the way a person looks and require medical and/or surgical treatment. Minor defects are abnormalities that do not cause serious health or social problems. When multiple birth defects occur together and have a similar cause, they are called syndromes. If two or more defects tend to appear together but do not share the same cause, they are called associations. . . .

Teratogens: Drugs, Chemicals, Radiation, and Infections

The specific cause of many congenital abnormalities is unknown, but several factors associated with pregnancy and delivery can increase the risk of birth defects.

Any substance that can cause abnormal development of the egg in the mother's womb is called a teratogen. In the first two months after conception, the developing organism is called an embryo; developmental stages from two months to birth are called fetal. Growth is rapid, and each body organ has a critical period in which it is especially sensitive to outside influences. About 7% of all congenital defects are caused by exposure to teratogens.

Only a few drugs are known to cause birth defects, but all have the potential to cause harm. For example, in 2003, a study found that use of topical (local) corticosteroids in the first trimester of pregnancy may be associated with cleft lip. Thalidomide is known to cause defects of the arms and legs; several other types also cause problems.

- *Alcohol.* Drinking large amounts of alcohol while pregnant causes a cluster of defects called fetal alcohol syndrome, which includes mental retardation, heart problems, and growth deficiency. In 2004, experts warned that binge drinking early in pregnancy was dangerous even if the woman quit drinking later.

- *Antibiotics.* Certain antibiotics are known tetratogens. Tetracycline affects bone growth and discolors the teeth. Drugs used to treat tuberculosis can lead to hearing problems and damage to a nerve in the head (cranial damage).
- *Anticonvulsants.* Drugs given to prevent seizures can cause serious problems in the developing fetus, including mental retardation and slow growth. Studies in the United Kingdom and Australia have tracked the percentage of birth defects caused by certain antiepileptic drugs.
- *Antipsychotic and antianxiety agents.* Several drugs given for anxiety and mental illness are known to cause specific defects.
- *Antineoplastic agents.* Drugs given to treat cancer can cause major congenital malformations, especially central nervous system defects. They also may be harmful to the health care worker who is giving them while pregnant.
- *Hormones.* Male hormones may cause masculinization of a female fetus. A synthetic estrogen (DES) given in the 1940s and 1950s caused an increased risk of cancer in the adult female children of the mothers who received the drug.
- *Recreational drugs.* Drugs such as LSD have been associated with arm and leg abnormalities and central nervous system problems in infants. Crack cocaine also has been associated with birth defects. Since drug abusers tend to use many drugs and have poor nutrition and prenatal care, it is hard to determine the effects of individual drugs.

Environmental chemicals such as fungicides, food additives, and pollutants are suspected of causing birth defects, though this is difficult to prove.

Drinking alcohol during pregnancy can cause a cluster of defects called fetal alcohol syndrome. (**Richard Newton/Alamy**)

Exposure of the mother to high levels of radiation can cause small skull size (microcephaly), blindness, spina bifida, and cleft palate. How severe the defect is depends on the duration and timing of the exposure.

Three viruses are known to harm a developing baby: rubella, cytomegalovirus (CMV), and herpes simplex. *Toxoplasma gondii*, a parasite that can be contracted from undercooked meat, from dirt, or from handling the feces of infected cats, causes serious problems. Untreated syphilis in the mother also is harmful.

Genetic Factors Are a Matter of Chance

A gene is a tiny, invisible unit containing information (DNA) that guides how the body forms and functions. Each individual inherits tens of thousands of genes from each parent, arranged on 46 chromosomes. Genes control all aspects of the body, how it works, and all its unique characteristics, including eye color and body size. Genes are influenced by chemicals and radiation, but sometimes changes in the genes are unexplained accidents. Each child gets half of its genes from each parent. In each pair of genes one will take precedence (dominant) over the other (recessive) in determining each trait, or characteristic. Birth defects caused by dominant inheritance include a form of dwarfism called achondroplasia; high cholesterol; Huntington's disease, a progressive nervous system disorder; Marfan syndrome, which affects connective tissue; some forms of glaucoma, and polydactyly (extra fingers or toes).

If both parents carry the same recessive gene, they have a one-in-four chance that the child will inherit the disease. Recessive diseases are severe and may lead to an early death. They include sickle cell anemia, [which is] a blood disorder that affects blacks, and Tay-Sachs disease, which causes mental retardation in people of eastern European Jewish heritage. Two recessive disorders that affect mostly whites are: cystic fibrosis, a lung and digestive disorder, and phenylketonuria (PKU), a metabolic disorder. If only one parent passes along the genes for the disorder, the normal gene received from the other parent will prevent the disease, but the child will be a carrier. Having the gene is not harmful to the carrier, but there is the 25% chance of the genetic disease showing up in the child of two carriers.

Some disorders are linked to the sex-determining chromosomes passed along by parents. Hemophilia, a condition that prevents blood from clotting, and Duchenne muscular dystrophy, which causes muscle weakness, are carried on the X chromosome. Genetic defects also can take place when the egg or sperm are forming if the mother or father passes along some faulty gene material. This is more common in older mothers. The most common defect of this kind is Down syndrome, a pattern of mental retardation and physical abnormalities, often including heart defects, caused by inheriting three copies of a chromosome rather than the normal pair.

A less understood cause of birth defects results from the interaction of genes from one or both parents plus environmental influences. These defects are thought to include:

- Cleft lip and palate, which are malformations of the mouth.
- Clubfoot, ankle or foot deformities.
- Spina bifida, an open spine caused when the tube that forms the brain and spinal cord does not close properly.
- Water on the brain (hydrocephalus), which causes brain damage.
- Diabetes mellitus, an abnormality in sugar metabolism that appears later in life.
- Heart defects.
- Some forms of cancer.

A serious illness in the mother, such as an underactive thyroid, or diabetes mellitus, in which her body cannot process sugar, also can cause birth defects in the child. In fact, in 2003, it was shown that babies of diabetic mothers are five times as likely to have structural heart defects as other babies. An abnormal amount of amniotic fluid may indicate or cause birth defects. Amniotic fluid is the liquid that surrounds and protects the unborn child in the uterus. Too little of this fluid can interfere with lung or limb development. Too much amniotic fluid can accumulate if the fetus has a disorder that interferes with swallowing. In 2003, a study linked the mother's weight to risk of birth defects. Obese women were about three times more likely to have an infant with spina bifida or omphalocele (protrusion of part of the intestine through the abdominal wall) than women of average weight. Women who were overweight or classified as obese also were twice as likely to have an infant with a heart defect or multiple birth defects than women classified as average weight.

FAST FACT

According to the Centers for Disease Control and Prevention, one of every thirty-three babies in the United States is born with a birth defect.

Various Diagnostic Methods

If there is a family history of birth defects or if the mother is over 35 years old, then screening tests can be done during pregnancy to gain information about the health of the baby.

- *Alpha-fetoprotein test.* This is a simple blood test that measures the level of a substance called alpha-fetoprotein that is associated with some major birth defects. An abnormally high or low level may indicate the need for further testing.
- *Ultrasound.* The use of sound waves to examine the shape, function, and age of the fetus is a common procedure. It also can detect many malformations, such as spina bifida, limb defects, and heart and kidney problems. In 2003, researchers in England announced a new combination of blood tests and ultrasound to detect Down syndrome sooner and more accurately than with the usual blood screenings done at 20 weeks of pregnancy.
- *Amniocentesis.* This test usually is done between the 13th and 15th weeks of pregnancy. A small sample of amniotic fluid is withdrawn through a thin needle

inserted into the mother's abdomen. Chromosomal analysis can rule out Down syndrome and other genetic conditions.

- *Chorionic villus sampling (CVS).* This test can be done as early as the ninth week of pregnancy to identify chromosome disorders and some genetic conditions. A thin needle is inserted through the abdomen or a slim tube is inserted through the vagina that takes a tiny tissue sample for testing.

If a birth defect is suspected after a baby is born, then confirmation of the diagnosis is very important. The patient's medical records and medical history may hold essential information. A careful physical examination and laboratory tests should be done. Special diagnostic tests also can provide genetic information in some cases. In 2003, the March of Dimes, a nonprofit organization, recommended that every baby born in the United States receive, at minimum, screening for the same core group of birth defects including phenylketonuria, congenital adrenal hyperplasia, congenital hypothyroidism, biotinidase deficiency, and others. They were concerned that newborn screening varied too much from state to state.

Treatment Often Depends on Specialized Attention

Treatment depends on the type of birth defect and how serious it is. When an abnormality has been identified before birth, delivery can be planned at a health care facility that is prepared to offer any special care needed. Some abnormalities can be corrected with surgery. Experimental procedures have been used successfully in correcting some defects, like excessive fluid in the brain (hydrocephalus), even before the baby is born. Early reports have shown success with fetal surgery on spina bifida patients. By operating on these fetuses while still in the womb, surgeons have prevented the need for shunts

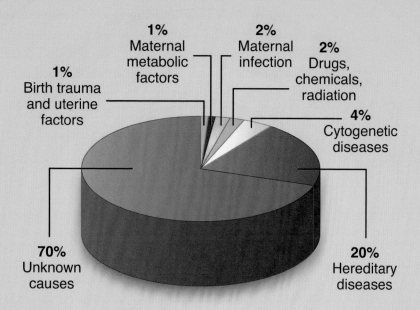

Most Birth Defects Have Unknown Causes

1%
Maternal metabolic factors

2%
Maternal infection

2%
Drugs, chemicals, radiation

1%
Birth trauma and uterine factors

4%
Cytogenetic diseases

70%
Unknown causes

20%
Hereditary diseases

Taken from: Karen Ericson and Teresa G. Odle, "Birth Defects," *The Gale Encyclopedia of Medicine*, 3rd edition. Ed. Jacqueline L. Longe. Detroit: Gale, 2006.

and improved outcomes at birth for many newborns. However, long-term studies still are needed. Patients with complicated conditions usually need the help of experienced medical and educational specialists with an understanding of the disorder. . . .

All Pregnant Women Can Follow Preventative Measures

Pregnant women should eat a nutritious diet. Taking folic acid supplements before and during pregnancy reduces the risk of having a baby with serious problems of the brain or spinal cord (neural tube defects). It is important to avoid any teratogen that can harm the developing baby, including alcohol and drugs. When there is a family history of congenital defects in either parent, genetic counseling and testing can help parents plan for future children. Often, counselors can determine the risk of a genetic condition occurring and the availability of tests for it. Talking to a genetic counselor after a child is born with a defect can provide parents with information about medical management and available community resources.

Common Birth Defects

Katrina Woznicki

In the following article Katrina Woznicki discusses the findings of a 2006 Centers for Disease Control and Prevention (CDC) report on the national incidence of birth defects. According to the report, cleft lip, cleft palate, and Down syndrome are the most common birth defects in the United States. The report suggests that the incidence of Down syndrome may be increasing, possibly because women are waiting longer to have children. However, more national research is needed before this can be confirmed, according to one of the report's authors. According to Woznicki, the CDC used data from eleven states to estimate the national incidence of common birth defects, including chromosomal defects; orofacial abnormalities; and cardiovascular, gastrointestinal, and eye defects. Woznicki is a nationally known health and medical writer.

Cleft lip and cleft palate, followed by Down's syndrome, remain the three most common birth defects, affecting almost 12,000 children altogether

SOURCE: Katrina Woznicki, "Orofacial Clefts and Down's Most Common Birth Defects," *MedPage Today,* January 6, 2006. www .medpagetoday.com. Reproduced by permission.

each year, CDC [Centers for Disease Control and Prevention] epidemiologists [in Atlanta] reported.

About 6,700 babies are born every year with orofacial deformities, and one out of every 733 live births results in a child with Down's syndrome, according to the CDC.

Down's Rates *May* Be Increasing

Previous estimates released by the National Down Syndrome Society indicated that trisomy 21 affected one of every 800 to one out of every 1,000 live births. This led to published reports suggesting that the CDC had found that Down's syndrome is becoming more common.

However, the CDC's Margaret Honein, Ph.D., said the report she and her colleagues published in the Jan. 6 [2006] issue of *Morbidity and Mortality Weekly Report [MMWR]* did not determine whether Down's syndrome rates are changing. This is because it is the first report to

A baby with a cleft lip and palate, the most common kind of birth deformity. (Dr. M.A. Ansary/Photo Researchers, Inc.)

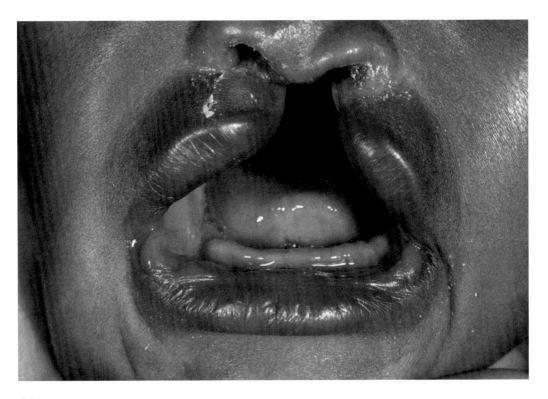

provide a relatively complete national picture of Down's syndrome based on population data.

Nevertheless, she said, it is possible Down's syndrome rates may be changing as more women postpone motherhood and push their biological clocks to the limit. "There certainly is a strong association between maternal age and Down's syndrome and the average maternal age has increased over the last few years," Dr. Honein said.

The estimated risk for Down's syndrome is about one in 1,000 for women who give birth under the age of 30, compared with a risk of one in 105 for 40-year-old mothers-to-be, the CDC said.

FAST FACT

Nearly 543,000 babies were born prematurely in 2006, according to the National Center for Health Statistics.

National Incidence of Birth Defects Based on State Data

The CDC report assessed the incidence of 18 out of the 45 most common birth defects, including orofacial abnormalities, Down's, hypoplastic left heart syndrome, musculoskeletal defects, and truncus arteriosus (also known as common truncus). The CDC did not include data on two common birth defects, spina bifida and anencephaly, because the agency said it already had solid national incidence data on these conditions.

State and local data indicate that 3% of all births in the United States are affected by birth defects. In the *MMWR* report, the authors looked at 1999–2001 National Birth Defects Prevention Network data from 11 states: Alabama, Arkansas, California, Georgia, Hawaii, Iowa, Massachusetts, North Carolina, Oklahoma, Texas and Utah.

Four states did provide data that included information from prenatal diagnoses of birth defects, Dr. Honein said. Whether those pregnancies ever resulted in abortion or miscarriage is unknown and lack of this kind of data from more states could affect overall national estimates.

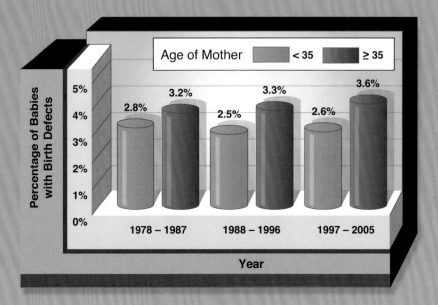

The Prevalence of Birth Defects Has Been Relatively Stable Since 1978

Age of Mother ▢ < 35 ▇ ≥ 35

Percentage of Babies with Birth Defects

1978 – 1987: 2.8%, 3.2%
1988 – 1996: 2.5%, 3.3%
1997 – 2005: 2.6%, 3.6%

Year

Taken from: Centers for Disease Control and Prevention, "Update on Overall Prevalence of Major Birth Defects— Atlanta, Georgia, 1978–2005," *Morbidity and Mortality Weekly Report*, January 11, 2008. www.cdc.gov/mmwr.

"We can improve birth defect surveillance by including those numbers to ascertain the number of affected pregnancies," she said.

Using data from these 11 states, the CDC was able to calculate national incidence estimates. Among the findings:

• Chromosomal defects affected 6,916 babies per year, including 5,429 with Down's syndrome alone. Based on the 11 states, the average incidence was calculated to be 12.94 per 10,000 live births a year. . . . Based on this data [and a margin of error], the national incidence was estimated to be 13.65 per 10,000 live births.

• Cleft lip with or without cleft palate affected 4,209 babies per year alone (cleft palate only affected 2,567 babies). The state data indicated an average incidence of 10.54 per 10,000 live births each year . . . and the national rate to be 10.48 per 10,000 live births.

• Cardiovascular defects affected a total of 6,257 babies per year whereas musculoskeletal defects affected 5,799 infants every year. For example, reduction defect of the upper limbs alone affected a total of 1,521 infants and was estimated to affect 3.84 of every 10,000 live births per year nationally.

• Gastrointestinal defects affected a total of 2,883 babies every year. For example, rectal and large intestinal atresia/stenosis was the most common defect in this category, affecting 4.84 babies out of every 10,000 lives births, according to state data and an estimated 4.81 babies out of 10,000 live births nationally.

• Eye defects were the least common, affecting a total of 834 babies every year. Anophthalmia/microphthalmia affected 2.09 per 10,000 live births every year, according to state data . . . and an estimated 2.08 per 10,000 live births nationally.

Better Monitoring of Data Could Help Prevent Birth Defects

Not all states monitor birth defect data, the CDC said, making it difficult for researchers to monitor the incidence of birth defects. Dr. Honein said the CDC intends to gather more data on this issue so that it can track any potential geographical hot spots in the U.S.

Additional research, she added, will also help clinicians better understand the causes of birth defects and could ultimately lead to prevention strategies, such as the campaign to encourage increased folic acid consumption, which led to a reduction in spina bifida.

Orthopedic Birth Defects May Have a Genetic Cause

Beth Miller

In the following article Beth Miller discusses research being done at Washington University in St. Louis that is focused on finding a genetic cause of orthopedic birth defects. So far, researchers have been unable to determine a specific cause for defects that affect the bones in the arms, legs, spine, hands, and feet. According to Miller, these are some of the most emotionally devastating birth defects because they are so physically obvious. Miller talks with Washington University researcher Christina Gurnett, who is analyzing the genes of several large families with a history of orthopedic defects. Gurnett hopes to find the genes responsible for these defects to help identify them and prevent defects from occurring. Miller is a senior medical news writer for Washington University in St. Louis.

Children can be sensitive to any physical difference they have from other children. But the patients that Christina Gurnett, M.D., Ph.D. studies are not just worried about having big ears, eyeglasses or

SOURCE: Beth Miller, "Researcher Seeks Genetic Cause for Orthopedic Birth Defects," *Washington University in St. Louis School of Medicine News and Information*, April 9, 2007. Reproduced by permission.

braces. Her patients have more emotionally devastating musculoskeletal disorders, including hands with more or less than five fingers, clubfoot and scoliosis.

Causes Are Unknown, but Defects Run in Families

Since the cause of these disorders and others like them is unknown, Gurnett, an assistant professor of neurology and pediatrics, is examining the possible genetic causes of these common disorders, which run in families.

Annual Estimates of Selected Birth Defects in the United States

Defects	Annual Number of Cases
Central Nervous System	
Anencephalus	1,009
Spina bifida without anencephalus	1,477
Cardiovascular	
Transposition of great arteries	1,901
Tetralogy of Fallot	1,574
Atrioventricular septal defect (also known as endocardial cushion defect)	1,748
Hypoplastic left heart syndrome	975
Orofacial	
Cleft lip with and without cleft palate	4,209
Cleft palate without cleft lip	2,567
Musculoskeletal	
Upper limb defect	**1,521**
Lower limb defect	**763**
Gastroschisis	1,497
Chromosomal	
Down syndrome	5,132

Note: Estimates based on pooled data from birth years 1999–2001.

Taken from: National Birth Defects Prevention Network, January 2009. www.nbdpn.org.

"As a neurologist, I want to take a new look at birth defects and the different genetic pathways that might be involved," Gurnett said. "Once we understand the underlying cause, we can work to find treatments for them."

To do so, Gurnett is evaluating the hundreds of children treated in St. Louis Children's Hospital's orthopedic clinic who have a congenital birth defect to search for a cause of their disorder.

"The orthopedic center sees 175 new patients a year with clubfoot, one of the most common birth defects, which affects one in 1,000 children," Gurnett said. "Twenty percent of those children have a family history of the disorder. We want to find markers or genes that will help develop an animal model so we can better understand what goes awry to cause these birth defects and ultimately figure out how to better treat and prevent them."

FAST FACT

According to the American Association of Orthopedic Surgeons, if one child in a family has clubfoot—a common orthopedic birth defect—the chance of a second child being born with clubfoot is about 5 percent.

Helping Fearful Families

One large family Gurnett is working with has a history of split hand malformation, a congenital limb malformation characterized by a deep cleft of the hand. Gurnett and her colleagues set up a genetics pedigree chart that shows which family members had the cleft hand.

"The third-generation women in this family are fearful of having children," Gurnett said. "We want to find the gene to help them determine their children's odds of having the disorder so we can find a way to prevent it. We may not find it the next day or the next week, but maybe in five to 10 years we will be able to use our advances in the lab to help patients in the clinic."

Another large family Gurnett is studying has 13 females with scoliosis. She and her colleagues examined each family member and collected DNA samples from 15 affected and 36 unaffected family members, and plan to

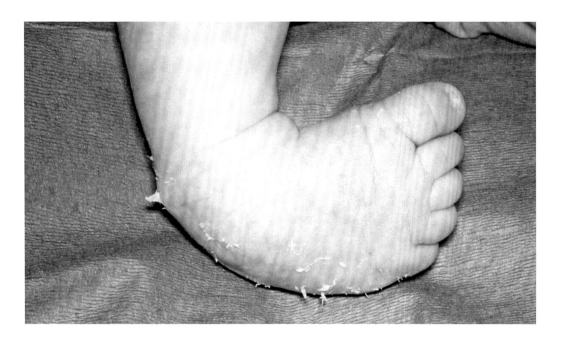

look for markers on chromosomes common to each of the women with scoliosis, then sequence the genes.

Gurnett is collaborating with Matthew Dobbs, M.D., associate professor of orthopaedic surgery. Together, they have established a DNA databank of musculoskeletal disorders that includes more than 700 DNA samples of patients with clubfoot; scoliosis; kyphosis, a curving of the spine that causes a bowing of the back, which leads to a hunchback or slouching posture; congenital vertical talus, a common cause of rigid flat foot; triphalangeal thumb, where the hand has another finger in place of a thumb; polydactyly, which causes the hands to have more than five fingers; and patients with other limb abnormalities.

Her research on limb development encompasses areas of critical importance in children's health, as these disorders severely impact quality of life and the mobility of children worldwide. Her work will provide a critical bridge between the rapid gains in genetic technology and the clinical need to answer biologically relevant questions in children with musculoskeletal disease.

Clubfoot in a newborn baby. One of the most common birth defects, it affects one in one thousand children. (Biophoto Associates/ Photo Researchers, Inc.)

The Environmental Causes of Structural Birth Defects

Betty Mekdeci and Ted Schettler

In the following article Betty Mekdeci and Ted Schettler provide information about potential links between environmental agents and birth defects. According to Mekdeci and Schettler, scientists must be very careful when studying the environmental causes of birth defects. Factors such as the timing of an environmental exposure and the large variation in human susceptibility to birth defects make it extremely challenging to unambiguously link the two together. Despite the difficulties, according to Mekdeci and Schettler, there are numerous scientific reports indicating that environmental agents such as certain medications, solvents, alcohol, pesticides, nicotine, and heavy metals can contribute to heart malformations, oral clefts, and other birth defects. The authors contend that more focused and systematic studies are needed to clarify the association between environmental agents and birth defects. Mekdeci is a cofounder of the nonprofit organization Birth Defect Research for Children. Schettler is a medical doctor and the science director at the Science and Environmental Health Network.

SOURCE: Betty Mekdeci and Ted Schettler, "Birth Defects and the Environment," The Collaborative on Health and the Environment, May 2004. Reproduced by permission.

S tudying the role that environmental factors play in causing birth defects is extremely challenging and current understanding is evolving. Research approaches include studies *in vitro* (test tube) and in laboratory animals, wildlife, and human populations.

Studying Environmental Causes of Birth Defects

Laboratory animal and in vitro *studies:* Animal studies are often used to examine whether or not an environmental agent may disrupt normal development. Such studies are required when a new drug or pesticide is proposed for the market, but these evaluations have significant limits. In general, they tend to emphasize obvious structural defects but are limited in their ability to identify functional defects. Species differences in susceptibility make it necessary to examine effects in at least two separate species. Genetic similarities in laboratory animals of the same species limit the value of this testing strategy for predicting impacts in genetically different populations of people. In short, the combined contributions of genetic, nutritional, and other environmental factors to birth defects in humans are not easily studied in laboratory animals. Nevertheless, animal studies continue to be extremely useful in identifying some agents that cause birth defects, sparing humans from unnecessary harm and suffering. Unfortunately, the developmental impacts of many commonly encountered industrial chemicals have not been studied at all, even in laboratory animals. *In vitro* screening techniques using dividing, living cells exposed to environmental agents avoid the use of laboratory animals and offer some promise for future directions.

Epidemiologic studies in human populations: Birth defect risks in human populations exposed to pharmaceuticals, drugs of abuse, pesticides, or other industrial chemicals can be studied using several different approaches. Each approach has its strengths and limitations.

Case reports may be useful when unusual defects suddenly show up in a cluster of children and are recognized by astute parents or clinicians. Investigation of the use of the drug thalidomide during pregnancy and the resultant severe arm and leg defects in children exposed prenatally is an example of an instance when case reports were helpful. Early suspicions of harmful effects were ignored in

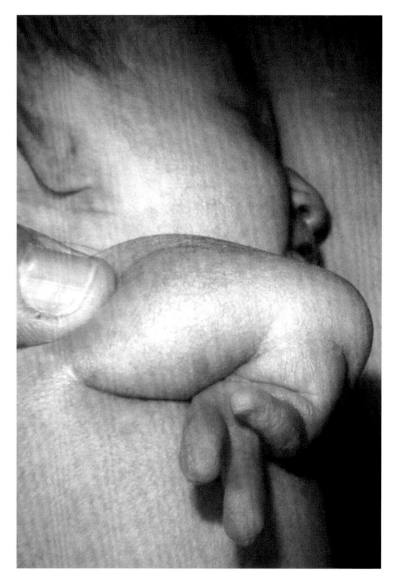

Limb reduction defects involve missing tissue or bone in part of a limb. (**Science Source**)

some countries, but case reports ultimately lead to case-control studies that confirmed the link, tragically only after a large number of children had been damaged. For a variety of reasons, however, investigations of case reports of clusters of defects may fail to find a cause, though they may generate hypotheses that warrant further study.

In another kind of study (cohort study) a large number of people are assigned to groups on the basis of chemical exposure or nutritional status, and pregnancy outcome is monitored. This kind of study is difficult, expensive to conduct, and rarely done. The National Collaborative Perinatal Project, launched in the 1950s, enrolled more than 50,000 pregnant women and followed them until their children were 8 years old. In this kind of study, many factors may contribute to pregnancy outcome and must be controlled for (e.g. family history, diet, occupation, smoking status, alcohol and drug use, etc).

Case-control studies are most commonly used to study the relationship between environmental factors and birth defects in people. In this kind of study, a group of children with a particular classification of defect is compared with a control group of children without the defect, but otherwise similar, to see if some difference in previous environmental exposures can be identified. This study design is often limited by inability to estimate accurately exposures that occurred months or years previously. Identification of the control group can also be difficult.

Major Challenges to Investigating Environmental Factors

Identifying, quantifying, and timing chemical exposures: Identifying, quantifying, and timing chemical exposures during fetal development are major challenges to investigating the role of environmental factors in causing birth defects. A large body of scientific research shows that not only the magnitude of exposure but also its timing is an extremely important determinant of risk because of the specific sequencing of developmental events. If the timing of potentially harmful exposures is not known, a link between birth defects and environmental factors may be missed. For example, children exposed to the drug thalidomide during the third to sixth week of gestation often suffered severe limb deformities, while children exposed later had either no or different health effects. Early exposures to thalidomide, approximately 20–24 days after conception, increased the risk of autism [according to toxicology expert Patricia Rodier].

Classifying birth defects: Regardless of study design, it is often difficult to know how best to group birth defects for analysis. There are tradeoffs among the choices. For example, in an attempt to increase the statistical power of a study to identify causal environmental factors by increasing the number of cases, researchers may "lump together" defects that should not be considered in the same category from the standpoint of developmental biology. "Heart defects," for example, are often considered to be a single category, but within this group are individual kinds of defects that should be considered individually. "Lumping" defects into a single category will tend to "hide" a specific defect that actually is causally related to a specific environmental factor. Yet, because individual defects are relatively rare, statistical power is lost when the number of cases is small.

Multifactorial causes of birth defects: Scientific evidence indicates that not all people are equally susceptible to birth defects. Genetic and nutritional factors may combine with other environmental factors to increase the risk. This combination of factors makes it extremely difficult to conduct epidemiologic studies in populations of people when the entire collection of risk factors is not well understood or identified.

Modest vs. dramatic increases in risks of birth defects: Some environmental agents appear to increase the risk of birth defects moderately but not dramatically. Though extremely important, modest increases in risk are difficult to demonstrate with a high degree of certainty and often remain unidentified. As a result, some reports of chemical agents that are known to cause birth defects are often limited to those that cause a large increase in risk. For example, some people argue that environmental agents should only be considered relevant and causally related to birth defects if they produce an increased risk of at least 6-fold. However, lesser increases in risks, for example, 1.5–2 fold, are also important and, in large populations, may result in considerable numbers of affected individuals. In numerous studies, many chemicals, or classes of chemicals, are implicated as significant contributors to the risk of birth defects, though the risk is frequently less than 6 times higher than in unexposed groups.

Some Examples of Environmental Exposures That Cause or Are Associated with Birth Defects

This section is based on published reports showing potential links between environmental agents and classes of birth defects in people. Laboratory animal data are not included in this section. This is an important limitation inasmuch as studies of the developmental impacts of chemical exposures are much more numerous in laboratory animals than in humans. Citations are obtained from searching Medline, Toxline, and medical textbooks.

It is important to recognize that, for some environmental agents, the evidence for a causal role in birth defects is strong whereas for others, the evidence is less consistent or weaker. For example, an increased risk of oral clefts associated with maternal smoking is much better established than other environmental risks for clefts. In some cases, studies that are not cited do not find the same associations, and additional investigations may or may not confirm the positive study's findings. A series of reports investigating the same agent or class of agents may have inconsistent or conflicting conclusions. For many, the best we can conclude is that available data "implicate" particular agents but further investigations are necessary to confirm the findings. This is the state of the science at the current time, highlighting the need for more systematic and focused attention, while at the same time asking when the weight of evidence is sufficient to act to protect health.

Heart Defects. Heart abnormalities are very common. Approximately 1 in every 400 newborns has a heart defect, [according to the California Birth Defects Monitoring Program]. Some heart defects such as holes in the heart wall may be mild and resolve without surgical intervention. Others like hypoplastic left heart syndrome are incompatible with life unless the baby can survive long enough to receive a heart transplant. . . .

Oral Clefts. Oral clefts are birth defects of the structures that form the mouth. A cleft lip means that the two sides of the upper lip did not grow together properly. A cleft palate is a split or opening in the roof of the mouth. Cleft lip and palate may occur individually or together in the same baby. The opening in the lip or palate may be on one side only (unilateral) or on both sides (bilateral). Oral clefts affect approximately one in every 700–1000 newborns with incidence variations in different racial groups. Families with a history of oral clefts in a parent, another child, or close relative, are more likely to have a baby with an oral cleft. But many families without such a history also have children with oral clefts. This had led researchers to believe that environmental factors can interact with specific genes to interfere with the patterns of normal palate closure and lip development. . . .

Neural Tube Defects (Anencephaly, Encephalocele, Spina Bifida). Neural Tube Defects (NTDs) are serious birth defects that involve incomplete development of the brain, spinal cord and/or the protective coverings of these organs.

Fetal Development and Timing of Air Pollution Risks

Legend: Dark blue bars indicate time periods when major morphological abnormalities can occur; light blue bars correspond to periods at risk for minor abnormalities and functional defects.

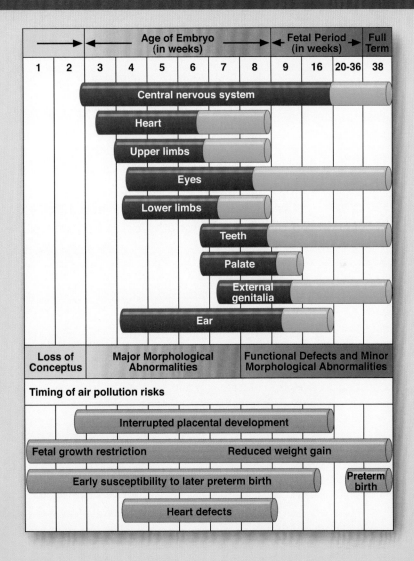

Taken from: Beate Ritz and Michelle Wilhelm, "Air Pollution Impacts on Infants and Children," *Southern California Environmental Report Card–Fall 2008*. UCLA Institute of the Environment, www.ioe.ucla.edu/reportcard.

There are three types of NTDs—anencephaly, encephalocele and spina bifida. Babies born with anencephaly have underdeveloped brains and incomplete skulls. Babies with encephalocele have a hole in the skull allowing brain tissue to protrude and babies with spina bifida have an opening in the spine that may allow part of the spinal cord to protrude. NTDs occur in one or two out of every 1,000 births. A family history of NTDs and maternal folate deficiency each increase the possibility of having a child with one of these defects, but most NTDs are believed to be multifactorial, meaning that they are likely to be caused by one or more genes interacting with an environmental factor. . . .

Limb Reduction Defects. Limb Reduction Defects (LRDs) involve missing tissue or bone in any part of a limb or limbs. LRDs can range in severity from missing fingers and toes to the complete absence of one or both arms and/ or legs. LRDs occur in about one out of every 2,000 births. Upper limb defects are twice as common as lower limb defects. Some LRDs are part of multiple birth defect syndromes that may be inherited. Many researchers believe, however, that the majority of LRDs are caused by the interaction of a susceptible gene and a triggering exposure. . . .

Understanding the Vulnerability of Embryonic and Fetal Development

Testing for developmental toxicity is an emerging science. Test methods are still undergoing development in laboratory animals and relatively few environmental chemicals have been examined for their ability to alter development in people. As a result, the functional impacts of fetal exposure to the large majority of environ-

FAST FACT

Women who lived within a quarter mile of a Superfund hazardous waste site during the first three months of pregnancy had a greater risk of having babies with heart defects and neural tube defects, according to a study by the California Birth Defects Monitoring Program.

mental chemicals on the immune, reproductive, nervous, and endocrine systems are unknown.

Considerable information does exist for a few environmental contaminants, showing that the fetus is commonly more sensitive to exposures than an adult. Exposures during developmental windows of susceptibility can have long-term and even life-long impacts, many of which are not detectable at birth.

The growing human brain, for example, is uniquely vulnerable to exposures to lead, mercury, manganese, polychlorinated biphenyls, alcohol, toluene, various other drugs of abuse, and pesticides. Animal studies confirm the unique susceptibility of the developing brain to these and other commonly encountered chemicals.

Similarly, the immature immune system is vulnerable to long-term disruption after exposure to some industrial and environmental chemicals. The field of developmental immunotoxicology is in its infancy, and there is little consensus surrounding the meaning of various changes in immune system parameters after fetal exposures. Based on available information, however, it is clear that developmental immunotoxicants can alter susceptibility to infection and other diseases, including allergies. . . .

Although more research will be necessary to clarify our understanding of details, the weight of current scientific evidence demonstrates the unique vulnerability of embryonic and fetal development to environmental exposures. Accumulated information indicates that the definition of "birth defects" must be expanded to include a much larger spectrum of structural and functional impacts, many of which are not apparent until years or decades after birth.

Birth Defect Prevention

Trust for America's Health

In the following article Trust for America's Health says there are many things women can do before they get pregnant that can prevent birth defects. According to the organization, women should maintain a healthy lifestyle and keep any chronic illnesses under control *before* getting pregnant in order to reduce the risks of birth defects. The organization notes that physicians and pharmacists play a key role in informing women about "preconception care," i.e., the things they should and should not do in their reproductive years, which can facilitate a healthy pregnancy and reduce the risks of birth defects. Trust for America's Health is a national nonprofit health-care organization.

Many health conditions and high-risk behaviors can be successfully managed or controlled before a woman becomes pregnant, increasing her chances of giving birth to a healthy baby. Preconception care is the strategy to reduce these risks.

SOURCE: Trust for America's Health, "Healthy Women, Healthy Babies," June 2008. Reproduced by permission.

Preconception Care

CDC [Centers for Disease Control and Prevention] and other groups have identified a series of established risks that can adversely affect pregnancy, and steps that can be taken *before* a woman becomes pregnant to reduce the chances of a bad outcome. There is considerable evidence that taking steps to address these risks well in advance of pregnancy will enhance the chances of having healthier babies. These include:

Diabetes management. Controlling blood sugar substantially reduces the threefold increase in birth defects among infants of diabetic women.

Obesity control. Reaching a healthy weight before becoming pregnant reduces the risk of neural tube defects, Cesarean section, hypertensive (high blood pressure) and thromboembolic (blood clots) disease that are associated with obesity.

Smoking cessation. Smoking is associated with premature delivery and low birth weight, among other things. It raises the risk of miscarriage, cleft lip or cleft palate, and problems delivering nutrition through the placenta, which is the source of the baby's nutrition and oxygen during pregnancy. A recent study also showed that mothers who smoke early in pregnancy are more likely to give birth to infants with heart defects. In addition to improving her own health, a woman can prevent these problems for her infant if she stops smoking before becoming pregnant. The 2004 Surgeon General's report found that only 18 percent to 25 percent of all women who smoke quit once they become pregnant. Too few primary care physicians use smoking cessation programs that have been shown to be effective as part of routine practice.

Eliminating alcohol abuse. Frequent or binge drinking is associated with fetal alcohol syndrome and other alcohol-related birth defects. Fetal alcohol syndrome is characterized by abnormal facial features, growth deficiencies, and central nervous system problems. Children

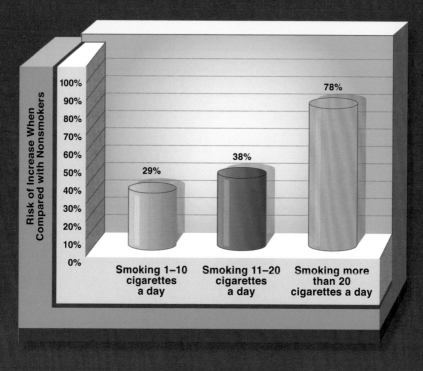

Maternal Smoking Increases the Risk of Finger and Toe Birth Defects

Risk of Increase When Compared with Nonsmokers

29% — Smoking 1–10 cigarettes a day

38% — Smoking 11–20 cigarettes a day

78% — Smoking more than 20 cigarettes a day

Taken from: Bio-Medicine, "Finger and Toe Abnormalities Related to Maternal Smoking," January 2006. www.bio-medicine.org.

born with fetal alcohol syndrome can have difficulties with learning, memory, attention span, communication, vision, hearing, or a combination of these. If a woman stops drinking before becoming pregnant, she can prevent these disorders in her baby. Studies have shown that primary care physicians can reduce frequent and binge drinking among women of childbearing age through brief, office- or clinic-based interventions.

Acutane use management. Acutane is a prescription medication for acne that can cause miscarriage and birth defects. Women who use this product and others in this class of drugs, known as isotretinoins, should stop before becoming pregnant. Pharmacists and physicians play a key role here.

Vaccinations. Women need protection against influenza, Hepatitis B and Rubella (commonly known as German measles), each caused by a virus. Vaccinations are available to prevent all of these illnesses. A pregnant woman with Hepatitis B (HBV) can transmit the infection to her fetus. Infection with HBV can cause liver damage, liver failure, liver cancer, and death. A Rubella infection in the mother can cause congenital rubella syndrome in her infant. This can result in serious birth defects.

Folic acid. Women of reproductive age should take folic acid supplements. Taking folic acid reduces by two-thirds the occurrence of defects in the neural tube, or fetal spinal column, the precursor to the central nervous system. Folic acid intake has increased since the FDA approved grain fortification; however, to prevent birth defects most women need to take a vitamin to supplement the folic acid they get from their diet.

Hypothyroidism management. Hypothyroidism occurs when the thyroid gland does not produce enough hormones. Hypothyroidism is treated by replacing the thyroid hormone the body needs. This is usually done with an oral tablet of the thyroid hormone thyroxine (T4 or levothyroxine). Adjusting the dosage of the drug early in pregnancy to higher levels will ensure proper neurological development in the fetus.

Maternal phenylketonuria (PKU). This is a genetic disorder characterized by the body's inability to process and use the essential amino acid, phenylalanine. Amino acids are the building blocks for body proteins. Women diagnosed with PKU as infants have an increased risk for delivering babies with mental retardation. However, this can be prevented when pregnant women follow a diet low in phenylalanine before conception and continue it throughout their pregnancy. (For example, avoiding high protein foods, such as meat, fish, poultry, eggs, cheese, milk, dried beans, and peas and eating measured amounts of cereals, starches, fruits, vegetables and a milk substitute.)

Anti-epileptic drugs. Certain drugs to treat epilepsy, a common chronic neurological disorder characterized by recurrent unprovoked seizures, are known teratogens, that is, agents that cause birth defects in a developing fetus. Valproic acid is one example. Women who must take these drugs for epilepsy control and want to become pregnant should be prescribed a lower dose. Again, both pharmacists and physicians play a key role in helping women understand risks and use appropriate medications.

Oral anticoagulant use management. Warfarin, a drug frequently used to control blood clotting, is a known teratogen, that is, a substance that causes birth defects. It is important for women who plan to become pregnant to switch to a safer drug before becoming pregnant.

HIV/AIDS screening and treatment. If HIV infection is identified before a woman becomes pregnant, she can take anti-retroviral medications to reduce the chances of transmitting the virus to her baby. Knowing in advance also provides an opportunity for women and/or couples to obtain additional information that can influence the timing of pregnancy and treatment.

STD (sexually transmitted diseases) screening and treatment. Chlamydia trachomatis and Neisseria gonorrhoeae are 2 sexually transmitted diseases that are strongly associated with ectopic pregnancy, which occurs when a fertilized egg has implanted outside the uterus, usually in a fallopian tube. These infections in the mother also can result in infertility and chronic pelvic pain. STDs during pregnancy can cause fetal death or substantial physical and developmental disabilities, including mental retar-

FAST FACT

One-fifth of American women are obese at the start of pregnancy, according to data from the Centers for Disease Control and Prevention's Pregnancy Risk Assessment Monitoring System.

dation and blindness. Early screening and treatment in the mother can prevent these dangerous outcomes.

Dental care. Emerging research points to a link between a mother's periodontal disease and premature birth for her infant. There also is a direct link between a mother's oral health and her offspring's risk for dental caries, or tooth decay. Women with high rates of dental caries should use fluorides and dietary measures to reduce the transmission of bacteria responsible for tooth decay.

To avoid birth defects and prematurity, women are urged to go through smoking cessation and alcohol abstinence programs before conception. **(Peter Erik Forsberg/ Alamy)**

Treating Birth Defects in the Womb

Claudia Kalb

In the following article Claudia Kalb says medical advances that allow surgeons to operate on fetuses while still in the womb have saved the lives of some children with life-threatening birth defects and have reduced the severity of non-life-threatening birth defects in other children. However, the procedures raise many moral and ethical questions. Chief among them is whose life is more important—the mother's or the child's? Fetal surgery has been performed to remove life-threatening tumors and repair spinal cords. According to Kalb, operating on fetuses with spina bifida is the most controversial of all the fetal surgeries because it is the only surgery performed that does not correct a life-threatening condition and its advantages are unclear. Kalb says scientists are doing studies to try to answer some of the questions that fetal surgery creates. Kalb is a general editor and a health, medicine, and science writer for *Newsweek*.

Samuel Armas, a chattering, brown-eyed 3-year-old, has no idea what "fetus" means. Nor does he realize that he was one of the most celebrated in medical history. At a mere 21 weeks of gestational age—long before it was time to leave his mother's womb—Samuel underwent a bold and experimental surgical procedure to close a hole at the bottom of his spinal cord, the telltale characteristic of myelomeningocele, or spina bifida. Samuel's parents, Julie and Alex, could have terminated Julie's pregnancy at 15 weeks when they learned about their son's condition, which can result in lifelong physical and mental disabilities. But the Armases do not believe in abortion. Instead, in August 1999, they drove 250 miles from their home in Villa Rica [Georgia] to Nashville [Tennessee], where Dr. Joseph Bruner, of Vanderbilt University, performed a surgery bordering on the fantastical. Bruner cut into Julie's abdomen, lifted her balloonlike uterus out of her body, made an incision in the taut muscle, removed the fetus, sewed up the spinal defect and tucked him back inside. Fifteen weeks later Samuel Armas "came out screaming," says Julie.

The Fetus as a Patient

That scream became a rallying cry for fetal-rights groups, which seized on a stunning photograph of Samuel's tiny hand emerging from his mother's uterus during surgery. Since then, anti-abortion activists have posted the image on dozens of Web sites to show just how real human fetuses are—even those that aren't yet viable. And that's just fine with the Armases. "We're very glad it's gotten visibility," says Alex. "That wasn't our fetus, that was Samuel."

No matter what legislators, activists, judges or even individual Americans decide about fetal rights, medicine has already granted unborn babies a unique form of personhood—as patients. Twenty-five years ago scientists knew little about the molecular and genetic journey from embryo to full-term fetus. Today, thanks to the biomedical revolution, they are gaining vast new insights into development, even envisioning a day when gene therapy will fix defects in the womb. Technology is introducing parents to their unborn children before they can see their toes. Expecting couples can now have amazing 3-D ultrasound prints made in chain stores like Fetal Fotos. "Instead of some mysterious thing inside her belly, a mother and her family can now identify a little human being," says Bruner. In any other field of medicine, the impact of these dramatic improvements in treatment and technology would be limited largely to doctors, patients and their families. But 30 long and contentious years after *Roe v. Wade* [the 1973 landmark case that legalized abortion in the United States], science that benefits fetuses cannot help but fuel ongoing political, moral and ethical debates.

Political, Moral, and Ethical Debates

Fetal surgery has raised the stakes to a whole new level. The very same tools—amniocentesis and ultrasound—that have made it possible to diagnose deformities early enough to terminate a pregnancy are now helping doctors in their quest to save lives. While fetal surgery is still rare and experimental, the possibility that a fetus that might have died or been aborted 10 years ago might now be saved strikes at the core of the abortion debate. And these operations also raise a fundamental question: whose life is more important—the mother's or the child's? While reluctant to take a stand in the political arena, doctors know they are players, like it or not. "We can be a lightning rod used to further a cause, either pro or con," says Diana Farmer, a fetal surgeon at the University of California, San Francisco [UCSF] "but you can't let that deter you from your mission as a physician."

For decades pediatric surgeons like Michael Harrison, head of UCSF's Fetal Treatment Center, agonized over their inability to save babies from deadly defects after birth. Since 1981, when Harrison performed a pioneering in utero procedure to treat a fetal urinary-tract obstruction, hundreds of fetuses have undergone treatments

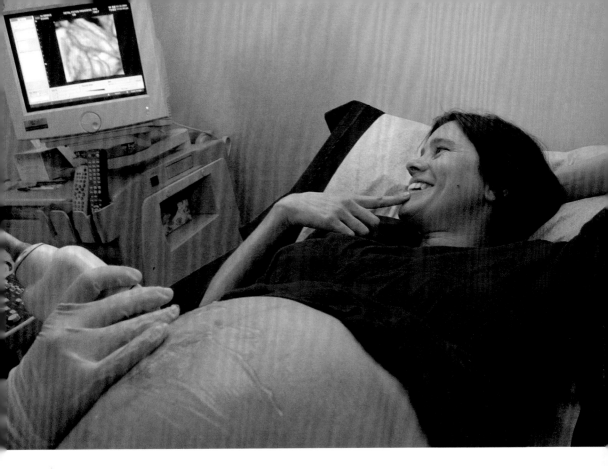

ranging from tumor removal to spinal-cord repair. Some operations have been dramatic successes, saving the lives of babies who would otherwise have died. Others have been heart-wrenching failures. In no other medical area are the stakes—two patients, not just one—so high. Now the first rigorous National Institutes of Health [NIH]–sponsored trials will put prenatal medicine, including the spina bifida procedure, to the test. "If there's not a clear advantage," says Farmer, "it's not worth putting the mother at risk."

On the streets, the womb has become a political battlefield. In the OR [operating room], it is a medical mine field. Fetuses are moving targets—just locating and positioning them is like trying to catch fish underwater. The placenta, the fetal lifeline, can develop anywhere in the uterus, obstructing access to the fetus. A single nick in the tissue can put the lives of both fetus and mother

A woman views a 4-D image of her unborn child displayed on a video monitor at Fetal Fotos in Pasadena, California. (**AP Images**)

in danger. Amniotic fluid, the liquid that cushions the growing fetus, can leak to perilously low levels. And pre-term delivery, which inevitably occurs because of the disruption to the uterus, is the Achilles' heel of fetal surgery, increasing a baby's likelihood of everything from lung problems to learning disabilities down the road. Bold and entrepreneurial by nature, fetal surgeons have endured the skepticism, even hostility, of colleagues for years. Early on, "folks thought we were nuts," says Dr. Scott Adzick, head of the Center for Fetal Diagnosis and Treatment at the Children's Hospital of Philadelphia (CHOP). "Some still do."

Fetal medicine has been tangled with politics from its inception. Harrison's predecessor in the field, New Zealander A. William Liley, is credited with the first successful fetal intervention in 1963, when he performed an in utero transfusion to treat Rh disease, a deadly blood incompatibility between mother and baby. But over the course of his career, he became as much activist as physician. Ardently opposed to abortion, Liley described the fetus as "a young human," and rallied for fetal rights until his death in 1983. While most doctors keep their beliefs private, the volatile confluence of politics and medicine has led some to join politically aligned groups like Pro-Life Maternal-Fetal Medicine, or Physicians for Reproductive Choice and Health. But those views can sway. In the past, right-to-life groups criticized surgeons for violating the sanctity of the womb. Now many support medical efforts to treat fetuses as patients. Such oscillations mean little to UCSF's Harrison. His goal from the beginning has been to deal with "the practical real problems of real people."

Susan and Jeff Dezurick are two such people. In October 1999, the couple learned that the twins Susan was carrying had a potentially deadly condition called Twin-

FAST FACT

According to the Centers for Disease Control and Prevention, birth defects are the number one cause of infant deaths, accounting for 136 deaths per 100,000 live births.

Twin Transfusion syndrome, in which one fetus floods the other with fluid through a shared blood vessel in the placenta. In a procedure called amnio reduction, the Dezuricks' doctors in Oakland [California], removed excess fluid from the saturated twin, hoping to ward off a buildup of pressure on his heart and lungs. But the technique, performed repeatedly on Susan, ultimately failed. With one of the twins on the verge of death, the Dezuricks arrived at UCSF. In a minimally invasive procedure, doctors located the culprit vessel, zapped it with a laser and cut off the faulty connection. (The two techniques—amnio reduction and laser—are now being compared in trials worldwide.) For the Dezuricks, the outcome was happy. Ten weeks after surgery, Sean and Christopher were born, premature but healthy. Today, lightly freckled 4-year-olds with impish grins, the boys spin around their living room, hugging each other on their tippy-toes. "Thank God for technology," says Susan.

Are the Benefits Worth the Risks?

As fetal science advances, the critical question remains: is the benefit to the fetus worth the risk to the mother? Ethicists can debate it all they like, but for Kristin Garcia, the answer was undeniably yes. In her 20th week of pregnancy, Garcia's doctor told her that her baby had a severe defect called congenital diaphragmatic hernia. "He told me that most women choose to terminate, because there's absolutely no way the baby would survive," says Garcia. At UCSF, doctors warned, as they do routinely, that they could not guarantee a positive outcome. In any procedure, risks to the fetus—which is usually operated on between 18 and 26 gestational weeks—include brain damage, physical deformities and death. The mother can suffer excessive blood loss or a permanently scarred uterus that could rupture in future pregnancies (C[esarean]-sections are done to avoid the problem), and, as with any major surgery, there is always the risk of death. For Garcia, the treatment was a success, but it was by no means easy. Fluid backed up into Garcia's lungs after the operation. "I couldn't breathe," she says. "I felt like I was dying." And little Analisa needed several surgeries to patch up her diaphragm. Today Analisa is "perfect and full of life," says Garcia. The physical and emotional tolls, however, were enormous. "I'm glad I did it for my first baby," says Garcia. "But I don't know if I could do it again."

As a lone female voice among fetal surgeons, Farmer is working hard to put the health of the mother front and center. Although fetal surgeries are rare—no more than about 600 patients are candidates in the United States in a given year—interest in the field is growing around the globe. At this year's [2003] annual fetal-surgery meeting, Farmer presented the first guidelines for maternal health, including a strict patient-consent process, counseling on nonsurgical alternatives and a fetal-oversight committee.

Even the best intentions for mother and baby cannot always save lives. Sherry Nicholson was almost 29 weeks pregnant when she and her husband, Phil, learned that their baby, Sean, had a lung mass that would almost certainly kill him in utero. The decision to try experimental surgery was "the only thing we could do," says Sherry. "I never wanted to wonder later 'what if?'" The operation went well, but 10 and a half weeks after delivery, Sean's healthy lung gave out and he died. Despite the tragic loss, Sherry is grateful for the outcome. "We got to know him and his personality," says Sherry. "He touched a lot of lives."

Of all of the fetal surgeries performed, the spina bifida operation is the most controversial. The disease, which affects one in 1,000 births every year, is the first and only condition surgeons have attempted to treat that is not life-threatening. And the advantages to going in so early are still unclear. Vanderbilt's Bruner has performed about 200 procedures since 1997 and his own results are mixed, but encouraging. Bladder and bowel function, vexing lifelong problems, do not appear to improve after intervention. But he says babies' brains show a clear benefit. Only about half need shunts—implantable devices that divert fluid from the brain—after birth, compared with the majority of babies operated on as newborns. Samuel Armas, who will soon have bladder surgery, cannot move his feet and toes, but he gets around fine with small leg braces. Not having a shunt, says Julie, "made the surgery worth it." The NIH trial, launched this spring

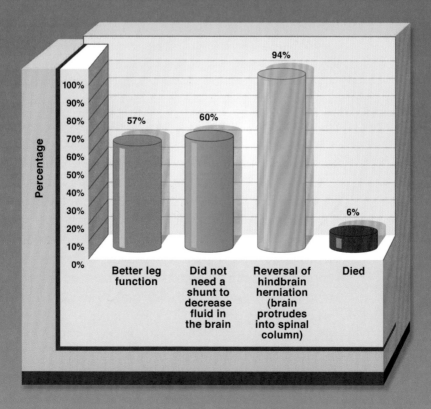

Outcomes of Fetal Spina Bifida Surgeries at the Children's Hospital of Philadelphia (1998–2002)

Taken from: *ScienceDaily*, "Fetal Surgery for Spina Bifida Shows Early Benefits in Leg Function, Fewer Shunts," October 1, 2003. www.sciencedaily.com.

[2003] at UCSF, CHOP and Vanderbilt, will recruit some 200 patients who will be observed until the age of 3. Doctors hope key questions will be answered: Is fetal surgery better than an operation after birth? And just how much benefit justifies the surgical risk?

Profound and Difficult Choices

In the end, no matter what the data show or the politicians decide, some fetuses will still turn out to be imperfect, and some parents will make choices they never thought possible. "I've had patients say to me, 'I marched up and down in front of [abortion] clinics, but I'm terminating my pregnancy,' says Dr. Mary Norton, head of prenatal diagnosis at UCSF. Andrea Merkord and her husband, Sean, do not believe in abortion. But last year Andrea had laser surgery to cut off the blood supply to a pair of conjoined babies in her uterus. The twins were unviable, but were threatening the life of a healthy triplet. That baby, Thomas, is now 7 months old and healthy. Andrea doesn't doubt her decision for a minute—but it continues to overwhelm her. "Obviously the twins were terminated and that is hard to say," she says in tears. "Until you've been in the situation, you don't know what decision you'll make."

For Vanderbilt's Bruner, operating on the tiniest patients has had a profound effect on his professional and personal life. Initially the experience was one of pure wonderment. "We would open the uterus and everything in the OR would stop. Everyone was just standing there looking." Now, Bruner says, he feels a deep and personal connection with every fetus. "I'm the first human being who will ever touch them," he says. "I speak to every one."

Controversies About Birth Defects

All Pregnant Women Should Have Prenatal Testing for Down Syndrome

The American College of Obstetricians and Gynecologists

In the following article the American College of Obstetricians and Gynecologists (ACOG) recommends that women of all ages be offered diagnostic testing for Down syndrome. Diagnostic tests such as amniocentisis and chorionic villus sampling (CVS) are invasive procedures that come with some risks to both mother and fetus. Previously, the ACOG recommended that women younger than thirty-five be offered less-invasive screening tests and not the more invasive diagnostic tests. However, the ACOG now says that scientific evidence indicates that women of all ages should be offered both screening and diagnostic tests for Down syndrome. The ACOG is a national nonprofit organization composed of professionals providing health care for women.

Photo on previous page. A doctor performs amniocentesis on a pregnant woman. The procedure assesses fetal stress or congenital defects such as Down syndrome. (John Watney/ Photo Researchers, Inc.)

A ll pregnant women, regardless of their age, should be offered screening for Down syndrome, according to a new Practice Bulletin issued today by The American College of Obstetricians and Gynecolo-

SOURCE: The American College of Obstetricians and Gynecologists, "Screening for Fetal Chromosomal Abnormalities," January 2007. Reproduced by permission.

gists (ACOG). Previously, women were automatically offered genetic counseling and diagnostic testing for Down syndrome by amniocentesis or chorionic villus sampling (CVS) if they were 35 years and older.

All Women Should Have the Option of Testing

The new ACOG guidelines recommend that all pregnant women consider less invasive screening options for assessing their risk for Down syndrome, a common disorder that is caused by an extra chromosome and can result in congenital heart defects and mental retardation. Screening for Down syndrome should occur before the 20th week of pregnancy.

A doctor administers a prenatal test for Down syndrome on a pregnant woman. (James King-Holmes/ Photo Researchers, Inc.)

"This new recommendation says that the maternal age of 35 should no longer be used by itself as a cut-off to determine who is offered screening versus who is offered invasive diagnostic testing," noted Deborah Driscoll, MD, a lead author of the document and vice chair of ACOG's Committee on Practice Bulletins-Obstetrics, which developed the Practice Bulletin with ACOG's Committee on Genetics and the Society for Maternal-Fetal Medicine.

ACOG also advises that all pregnant women, regardless of their age, should have the option of diagnostic testing. ACOG recognizes that a woman's decision to have an amniocentesis or CVS is based on many factors, such as a family or personal history of birth defects, the risk that the fetus will have a chromosome abnormality or an inherited condition, and the risk of pregnancy loss from an invasive procedure.

Guidelines Are Based on Scientific Evidence

According to the new guidelines, the goal is to offer screening tests with high detection rates and low false positive rates that also provide patients with diagnostic testing options if the screening test indicates that the patient is at an increased risk for having a child with Down syndrome. Because of the number of multiple screening strategies currently available, the document provides ob-gyns with some suggested screening strategies that they can choose to offer in their practice to best meet the needs of their patients. The guidelines discuss the advantages and disadvantages of each screening test and some of the factors that determine which screening test should be offered, including gestational age at first prenatal visit, number of fetuses, previous obstetrical and family history, and availability of various screening tests.

> **FAST FACT**
>
> According to the National Institutes of Health, about 75 percent of babies with Down syndrome are born to women older than thirty-five.

Weighing the Risks of the Mother's Age

The risk of pregnancy with Down syndrome and other chromosomal abnormalities increases sharply with the age of the mother. New guidelines urge all pregnant women, not just those over thirty-five, to be screened.

Risk of Down Syndrome

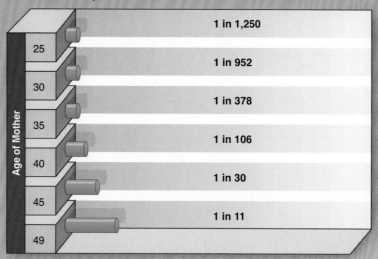

Risk of All Chromosomal Disorders, Including Down Syndrome

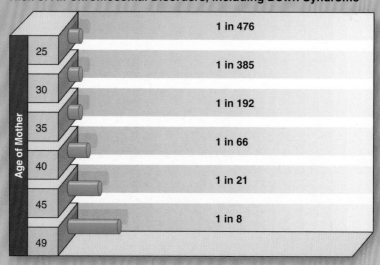

Taken from: Roni Rabin, "Screen All Pregnancies for Down Syndrome, Doctors Say," *New York Times*, January 8, 2007. www.nytimes.com.

The following ACOG recommendations are based on good and consistent scientific evidence:

- First-trimester screening using both nuchal translucency (NT), an ultrasound exam that measures the thickness at the back of the neck of the fetus, and a blood test is an effective screening test in the general population and is more effective than NT alone.
- Women found to be at increased risk of having a baby with Down syndrome with first-trimester screening should be offered genetic counseling and the option of CVS or mid-trimester amniocentesis.
- Specific training, standardization, use of appropriate ultrasound equipment, and ongoing quality assessment are important to achieve optimal NT measurement for Down syndrome risk assessment, and this procedure should be limited to centers and individuals meeting this criteria.
- Neural tube defect screening should be offered in the mid-trimester to women who elect only first-trimester screening for Down syndrome.

Prenatal Testing Should Not Be Expanded to All Women

Victoria Seavilleklein

In the following article Victoria Seavilleklein asserts that expanding prenatal testing to all pregnant women, regardless of age, is not warranted. According to Seavilleklein, one of the primary arguments used in favor of expanding prenatal testing is that it supports a woman's free choice, or autonomy. However, Seavilleklein argues, this is not true. She believes that women are not being given adequate information about prenatal testing and that this inadequacy undermines their informed consent. She also introduces the concept of relational autonomy and contends that the choice to undergo prenatal testing is not decided independently by each woman but is instead impacted by many outside factors. According to Seavilleklein, myriad social, political, and cultural factors persuade women to have prenatal testing, in essence reducing their own independent choice. Seavilleklein does not think that offering prenatal testing to women younger than thirty-five increases women's autonomy, and for this reason she does not believe it should be offered to all women routinely. Seavilleklein is clinical and organizational ethics fellow at the University of Toronto, Joint Centre for Bioethics.

SOURCE: Victoria Seavilleklein, "Challenging the Rhetoric of Choice in Prenatal Screening," *Bioethics*, vol. 23, 2009, pp. 68–77. Copyright © 2009 Basil Blackwell Ltd. Reproduced by permission of Blackwell Publishers, conveyed through Copyright Clearance Center, Inc.

Prenatal screening in Canada is on the verge of expanding in multiple different directions. This screening, consisting of maternal serum screening and nuchal translucency screening, is designed to identify pregnant women likely to have fetuses with chromosomal anomalies and open neural tube defects; once identified, these women can be offered further diagnostic testing with the option of abortion if test results are positive. While prenatal screening has traditionally been limited to pregnant women considered to be 'high-risk', the Society of Obstetricians and Gynaecologists of Canada (SOGC) has recently recommended that it be offered to all pregnant women regardless of age, disease history or risk status. Similar recommendations have been made by the American College of Obstetricians and Gynecologists (ACOG). In addition to broadening the target population of screening, the number of conditions being screened for is likely to increase. For decades, prenatal screening has been used to screen for Down syndrome, open neural tube defects, and Trisomy 18. Current studies, however, show that prenatal screens might also be used to detect conditions such as Smith-Lemli-Opitz syndrome, Trisomy 13, Turner's syndrome, and cystic fibrosis. Hence, this particular juncture is an ideal moment to pause and reflect on the reasons for this proliferation of screening and the values that it is deemed to support.

Women's Autonomy Is Used to Support Prenatal Testing

One of the principal values that is offered in support of prenatal screening is autonomy. The value of autonomy, often framed in terms of women's choice, is widely recognized by those who fund, research, develop, and implement prenatal screening and is central in obstetrics and genetics departments and public information pamphlets. Even those who object to some or many aspects of prenatal screening, such as disability rights activists, prioritize autonomy when they state that decisions about the kind of children one will raise—if such decisions must be made at all—are better left to individual women than to society or the medical profession. In this paper, I critically examine the value of autonomy in the context of prenatal screening to determine whether it justifies the expansion of prenatal screening to all pregnant women. I argue that current screening practice does not protect or promote women's autonomy in the vast majority of cases, either on a narrow analysis of choice reflecting individual autonomy or on a broad analysis of choice reflecting relational autonomy. Consequently, we should hesitate before expanding screening to more pregnant women.

The value of autonomy is deeply entrenched in contemporary society. It is a reflection of broad social-political change brought about in the second half of the 20th century by second-wave feminism, the civil rights movement in the US, and the development of the Charter of Rights and Freedoms in the new Canadian Constitution. It also represents efforts to distance current genetics practices from the coercive and discriminatory practices of past eugenics movements and from other abuses in human experimentation and clinical medicine.

Women Are Not Making Informed Choices

Despite its importance in society and particularly in genetics, there is incontrovertible evidence that women are not making free informed choices about prenatal screening. Autonomy is protected in health care by the theory and practice of informed consent, the most authoritative and widely disseminated theory of which is described by Tom Beauchamp and James Childress. In a specific decision-making context, informed consent is deemed to be reached if the person is competent, if adequate standards of disclosure and understanding about the intervention are attained, and if consent (i.e. authorization) is given voluntarily. According to studies conducted in North America and in the Western world, informed consent is not being met in the vast majority of cases in prenatal screening. In particular, a recent Health Technology Assessment, conducted by Green et al. for the UK's [United Kingdom's] National Health Service, identified and surveyed 78 studies that have been conducted internationally about the psychosocial implications of prenatal screening. Most of these studies were conducted in the US and the UK, although several are from Canada and other European countries. The overwhelming conclusion drawn from all of this research concerned 'the inadequacy of current procedures for achieving informed consent'.

There is no one element of informed consent that consistently fails to achieve an adequate threshold level in prenatal screening. Rather, any of disclosure, understanding, voluntariness and consent can be challenged as inadequate in light of the empirical evidence of current practice. I will give some examples of each. . . .

Disclosure Inadequate

Disclosure is important because its quality determines women's ability to understand the test. The SOGC recommends that the following information be provided to pregnant women prior to a screening test:

> details about the conditions being screened, the likelihood of detection, the method of screening, the meaning of a screen-positive result and a screen-negative result, the choices following a screen-positive result (amniotic fluid alpha fetoprotein, acetylcholinesterase and fetal karyotype, detailed ultrasound for fetal anomaly), the choices following a positive diagnosis (abortion or continuation of the pregnancy) and details as to how further information can be obtained.

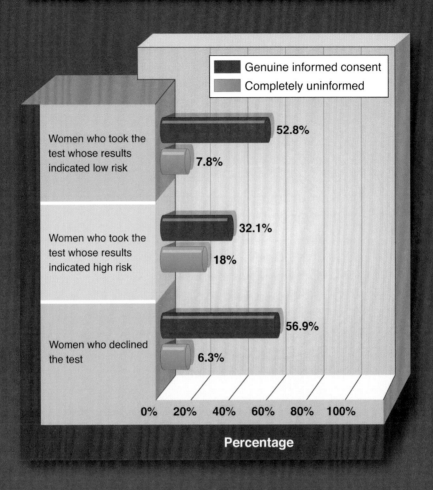

The Level of Informed Consent for a Prenatal Screening Test in France

- ■ Genuine informed consent
- ▨ Completely uninformed

Women who took the test whose results indicated low risk
- 52.8%
- 7.8%

Women who took the test whose results indicated high risk
- 32.1%
- 18%

Women who declined the test
- 56.9%
- 6.3%

0% 20% 40% 60% 80% 100%

Percentage

Taken from: Romaine Favre et al., "What About Informed Consent in First Trimester Ultrasound Screening for Down Syndrome?" *Fetal Diagnosis and Therapy*, 2008.

While full counselling is not recommended, this still encompasses a great deal of information to disclose in a short clinical encounter. Describing the details of the conditions screened for alone will take several minutes. Nevertheless, a 1993 report of the Royal Commission on New Reproductive Technologies revealed that physicians spent less than five minutes on average discussing maternal serum screening. A US study reported a discussion time of approximately two minutes. This is a very limited period of time in which to disclose all the relevant material listed by the SOGC. In practice, relevant details are often disclosed incorrectly to pregnant women, not disclosed at all (such as the possibility of abortion if consequent tests are positive), or a discussion does not even take place.

In health care, patients must not only be given information relevant to their decision-making, they must also understand the information that they have been given. Full understanding is not required for informed consent but patients should understand the salient aspects of the proposed procedure and the consequences of proceeding with the intervention or not. Studies evaluating women's knowledge and understanding of prenatal screening overwhelmingly show that women do not understand the testing, including basic facts such as why the test is being done, what conditions are being looked for, what the results mean, and what will (or may) follow after testing. These findings are the same both for women who choose to have testing and for those who decline. . . .

Voluntariness Is Undermined

Once the relevant information has been disclosed and understood, a decision must be made voluntarily, or in the absence of a substantially controlling influence. Whether an act is controlled, non-controlled, or somewhere in between depends on the degree to which a patient acts on the basis of her own will. The most obvious cases where voluntariness is undermined are when women are not asked for their authorization at all or when they believe that testing is mandatory. . . .

The influence that a health-care provider has on a woman's decision-making is widely recorded in the literature on prenatal diagnosis, with decision-making correlating with factors such as the provider's approach, gender, and specialty (i.e. obstetrician versus general practitioner).

This same trend has been observed in prenatal screening. [Medical anthropologists] Nancy Press and Carole Browner found that the very diverse group of women in their study—who almost unanimously accepted screening—were influenced primarily by the way in which the screening was described to them by their health-care provider and in patient information pamphlets (both of which were biased in favour of screening). [Political scientist] Diane Paul goes so far as to say that the strongest determining factor in whether women choose to have screening is not in the attitudes of the women but in the approach taken by their health-care provider. Whether this influence is sufficient to undermine voluntariness may be debated. However, in some cases, health-care providers may use their influence to more directly determine the choices of pregnant women. For instance, concerns about litigation, if women do not have screening and end up having a child with a disability, may cause some physicians to err on the 'safe' side and convince women to have screening in a way that may be regarded as substantially controlling.

Consent Not Always Asked

Consent, the final element, refers to the authorization given for a specific procedure or intervention to be performed. It can be express, tacit (given through silence or by omission), implicit or implied (when consent is interpreted by certain actions), or presumed (based on assumptions of what a person will or should do). It is clear from documents on prenatal screening that the form of consent considered to be appropriate is express consent. . . . The empirical evidence discussed above shows that express consent for prenatal screening is not always asked for or given by women undergoing the testing.

Hence, while some health-care providers may be very skilled at clearly disclosing the relevant information and some pregnant women may understand the test sufficiently to provide express voluntary consent (or refusal), in the majority of cases adequate levels of informed consent are not being achieved. Given the importance of autonomy in our society and in genetics in particular, it is essential that efforts be made to improve the process of informed consent in order to protect free informed choice for pregnant women. The fact that reproductive autonomy is not being well protected in current prenatal screening practice should also make us wary about expanding the scope of screening to pregnant women population-wide.

Look at Relational Autonomy

Even if the process of informed consent were improved, however, this theory reflects a very narrow conception of choice; it reflects a bias in the literature about choice traditionally understood as individual choice, or individual autonomy, in a specific decision-making context. An analysis of women's choice is thereby restricted to their ability to accept or decline a particular option that is offered to them. It allows no room for reflection on the practice that is making those particular choices available or on other contextual influences outside the clinic that may not qualify as coercive or substantially controlling but may nevertheless have a significant impact on women's decision-making. If prenatal screening is intended to represent something more than an additional consumer choice for women, then a broader conception of choice is required.

> **FAST FACT**
>
> The risk of miscarriage due to amniocentesis prenatal testing is about one in sixteen hundred, according to a 2006 study reported in the journal *Obstetrics & Gynecology.*

A broader conception of choice requires a different kind of theory. In traditional theories of autonomy, persons are characterized as independent, self-sufficient, rational decision-makers who can receive information and make decisions by weighing the costs and benefits of various options. By contrast, in theories of relational autonomy, persons are viewed as relational beings embedded within and shaped by a web of interconnected relationship. As a result of this conception of selves, persons, and their values, desires, etc. are seen as constructed in part by their social environment. Relational autonomy (understood in a broad sense) has a much larger scope than informed consent, or individual autonomy. It explicitly includes consideration not only of women's decision-making in the clinic, but also of the social and political context in which practices develop and choices are offered; it is not just the quality of the information disclosed to pregnant women that matters but the kinds of choices that are available, how these choices are framed, and what opportunities or pressures women experience as a result. These contextual features, illuminated by a relational approach, provide additional reason to challenge the claim that prenatal screening should be promoted and expanded on the basis of autonomy.

Screening Was Not Developed with Women in Mind

Contextual factors, such as the research agenda, political and economic interests, and historical circumstance, are worth exploring because they provide insight into the practice of prenatal screening and determine the choices that women will face in the clinic. [French sociologist] Carine Vassy argues that in the UK prenatal screening was not developed in response to the demands of women, as is often claimed, but that programs were initiated by government organizations, interested sectors of the medical profession, and the medical supply industry for their own purposes. . . .

Similarly, despite the rhetoric of choice in screening programs and the conviction of clinicians that 'women want this testing' and that 'we are just offering women what they want', there is little support in the literature for women driving the initiative to develop and implement prenatal screens; this creative impetus seems to have come from elsewhere. . . .

The Value of Technology

Once prenatal screening is established, its implementation and uptake may be propelled by cultural attitudes about the value of information and of science. 'Information is power', 'more information is better than less', and 'information increases choice' are all familiar mantras. The emphasis on informed choice that is pervasive in prenatal screening seems to reinforce this view. For example, in a study conducted by Press and Browner of Catholic pregnant women, the participants thought it was better to have the information about a positive screen result despite the fact that nothing could be done about it (or would be done about it, since most did not want to abort). Moreover, the belief appeared to be unanimous that scientific information 'could not, or should not, be refused.' . . .

Whether more information, obtained via new screening options, will increase choice is also unclear. [Sociologist] Barbara Katz Rothman explains that sometimes new options quietly foreclose on old possibilities. . . .

When the focus of society is on a new option, such as prenatal screening, other possibilities might become harder to choose or may silently disappear. In other words, once women exercise their ability to make the choice to use prenatal screening, they might lose their ability not to choose it! . . .

Social, Political, and Cultural Forces

Social-political forces and entrenched cultural assumptions can also affect how choices are framed and how free women may feel to make certain decisions. For instance, recommendations for the widespread offering of amniocentesis were instigated by two major lawsuits filed (and won) by women who had not been offered testing and had given birth to children with disabilities. Because of the fear that any problems with a newborn must be assigned a culprit, clinicians may be worried that even if a woman does not wish for screening now, in retrospect, she might have wanted it, in which case clinicians may be liable. As a result, health-care providers may be more persuasive when offering a test than strict standards of disclosure would allow and make it hard for women to decline screening.

The language used to describe the screening may also affect choice. For example, disability rights activists have challenged the use of language such as 'abnormalities', 'defects', and 'risks' because they are normative and have built-in negative connotations. Women's decisions may be subtly influenced by how they interpret these terms. Language may also mislead when comments referring to screening as a way to 'make sure your baby is healthy' imply that testing is meant to ensure health rather than to detect certain conditions. . . .

Entrenched cultural assumptions about the roles and responsibilities of women and mothers may increase the difficulty women face in refusing screening. [Health and social studies professor] Abby Lippman argues that claims that women themselves need or choose prenatal screening is something constructed by the context of testing. The fact that women are generally responsible for the health of the family and that screening is often por-trayed as part of routine prenatal care makes screening seem like the responsible course to take. . . .

The labelling of pregnant women as 'at-risk' is also likely to construct a perceived need for testing according to Lippman. A woman labelled 'high-risk' may feel that she requires testing in order to reduce her risk, whatever her actual risk figure. Indeed, in pregnancy, everyone is categorized as 'at-risk'; they are either low or high risk, at least until all the results are in. No one is 'no-risk' de-spite the fact that the vast majority of children are born healthy and at term. Because of the negative and fearful connotations of risk, the label of risk may make women feel more dependent on technology for their pregnancies to reduce this risk and to provide reassurance that their pregnancy is progressing normally. . . .

Hence, the existence of the technology and the way it is portrayed creates the perception that it is a necessary part of prenatal care, not merely an optional one. Once screening becomes even more normalized, it may not even be reassuring to be in a low risk bracket or to have one's risk reduced; the impetus for testing may remain due to the fact that fears over the conditions being screened for may become enhanced due to the constant public focus created by prenatal screening and diagnosis. Also, as tests become more normalized, they become harder to question or decline and they become part of the care that is desired by women and expected of women. . . .

Why This Choice and Not Others?

A framework of relational autonomy also allows us to look beyond the available choices to consider other possibilities. The choice that is being offered with prenatal screening is not the choice to have a blood test but the choice to avoid having a child with a certain condition, primarily one that could result in a disability. Prenatal screening is the first step in offering women this choice. Why is this choice being supported and not others? For example, women can choose to abort a fetus with Down syndrome or spina bifida at 20 weeks gestation but they cannot choose to abort a fetus at 20 weeks based on fetal sex (in the absence of a sex-linked disorder). Abortions on the basis of fetal sex are considered to be morally objectionable because of entrenched sex discrimination against female fetuses; hence, abortions based on this trait are not supported by the medical profession. Nor is it widely supported for women to choose to give birth under water or using a birthing stool, to give birth at home, or to stay several days in the hospital after labour in order to have time to rest and adjust to being a mother. In other words,

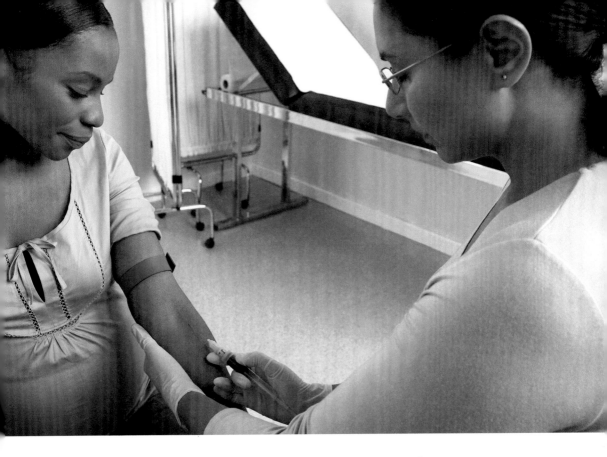

Social, political, and cultural factors influence a woman to undergo prenatal testing. **(Adam Gault/ Photo Researchers, Inc.)**

it is only possible to make choices about a narrow range of options that are defined by the medical system. Whether certain options will be available to pregnant women depends on the eligibility criteria set by the medical system, and these occasionally shift in light of professional practice guidelines as is the case with prenatal screening. Likewise, prenatal technologies are not freely available for women to choose but can only be accessed through the medical system acting as gatekeeper. . . .

Many Factors May Restrict Ability of Women to Make Free Choices

In summary, there are a multitude of factors in society that might influence women's choices in the clinical context; while these factors might not be characterized as coercive or substantially controlling, as described in the theory of informed consent, they may nevertheless restrict the ability of women to make a free choice in the face of screening options. These forces include the normalization of technology combined with a cultural desire for information, cultural assumptions about women and mothers being responsible for health combined with the misperception of medical technology as promoting the birth of a healthy child, the categorization of pregnant women into risk categories with technology offering risk reduction and reassurance, and medical and societal values that determine which choices will be supported and made available to pregnant women. Hence, a broader conception of choice using a relational framework reveals additional reasons to worry that the expansion of prenatal screening may undermine women's autonomy.

To be clear, I am not advocating that prenatal screening be withheld from pregnant women. Reproductive autonomy is highly valued in our society and is important because of past coercive practices in reproduction and continued gender oppression. Because having a child with a disability may have a significant impact on a woman's life (depending on the severity) and because she is more likely to be responsible for the care work, she is in the best position to judge whether having a child with a disability is something that she could manage. However, it is not clear that women are being given the opportunity to make informed choices about screening. Some women are being subtly directed down a path that, given greater understanding, they might not have chosen. Increased normalization through the continued expansion of prenatal screening will extend these concerns to all pregnant women. In order to promote reproductive autonomy for women who want testing while protecting the autonomy of women who may not, alternative means of implementing prenatal screening should be pursued. One possibility that I explore elsewhere is to make screening available to all women who want it without routinely offering it as part of standard prenatal care.

Broadened Prenatal Screening Is Not Warranted

In short, whether choice is interpreted narrowly as informed consent or broadly as relational, there are reasons to worry that women's autonomy is not being protected or promoted by the routine offer of screening. At minimum, efforts must be made to improve the process of informed consent, which is no easy task. Steps should also be taken to address some of the contextual factors that restrain choice. In the meantime, however, incorporating the offer of prenatal screening into routine prenatal care for all pregnant women is not supported by the value of autonomy and ought to be reconsidered.

Plastic Surgery to Correct Down Syndrome Facial Features Is Unethical

Ann K. Suziedelis

In the following article Ann K. Suziedelis argues that putting a child with Down syndrome through cosmetic surgery to make him or her appear more "normal" is unethical. Suziedelis examines the ethicality of cosmetic surgery for two children: "Lili," who has a large hemangioma removed from her face; and "Jimmy," who has Down syndrome and undergoes surgery to make his face appear more like that of children without Down syndrome. She concludes that Lili's surgery is justifiably ethical because her hemangioma is an incidental factor in who she is as a person. However, Suziedelis concludes that Jimmy's cosmetic surgery is unethical primarily because it leaves him without a set of peers that are truly like him. According to Suziedelis, Jimmy should not be changed to fit in with society; rather, society should change to accept Jimmy the way he is. Suziedelis is a bioethicist and is vice president of Mission and Ethics at St. Joseph Mercy Oakland Hospital in Pontiac, Michigan.

SOURCE: Ann K. Suziedelis, PhD, "Cosmetic Surgery for Children with Down Syndrome: The Cruelest Cut of All?" *Health Care Ethics USA,* vol. 11, 2003. Reproduced by permission.

Two television documentaries aired recently [2003] featuring pediatric plastic surgeons and their small patients. The first involved "Lili," who suffered from a deep red, tumor-like hemangioma, the size of a hen's egg, which sat prominently on her cheek. It was successfully removed, and we saw her several months later, with only a faint scar where the growth had been. She was playing with other children, her now beautifully unspectacular face blending in among theirs.

The other story was about four-year-old "Jimmy," a boy with Down Syndrome [DS], whose parents opted to alter his facial features surgically, so that he would look more 'normal.' (The word 'normal' is problematic, and it is used here in its most common sense, i.e., conforming to the average in a large group.) Jimmy, of course, already looked quite normal for a boy with Down Syndrome, so the actual goal of the surgery was to make him look more like a child without Down Syndrome. We were introduced to him as he played with friends, while his parents discussed the upcoming surgery. The procedure was performed (as was Lili's) under general anesthesia. It included resection of his tongue, lifting of the bridge of his nose, removal of fat from his neck, placement of implants in his cheekbones, and removal of the distinctive folds of his eyelids. He was also shown, some time later, playing happily with friends.

While there are other children with Down Syndrome or hemangiomas who undergo similar operations for therapeutic reasons, it is important to make clear that Lili's and Jimmy's were, from a physical perspective, purely cosmetic. Leaving aside surgical procedures undertaken to improve or restore a child's physical functioning, and considering only those carried out solely for cosmetic reasons, questions arise of whether they are ever ethically justifiable, and if Lili's and Jimmy's are ethically equivalent.

Principles of the Human Community

These two children clearly have physical and intellectual differences, but as human persons they also have much in common. For example, the principle of totality and integrity requires them to develop, use, care for, and preserve all of their natural physical and psychic functions. It directs us all to respect the gifts given to us by God, as well as those given to every other person, so that mutual dignity can be fostered within the human community. This dignity is neither variable nor subjective, for we are willed by God and imprinted with God's image. The dignity we possess stems not from our personal attributes—our beauty, our brains, our talents or skills—but from the persons we are as children of God. Further, we are not only sacred but social. We live in society, and each of us is called to consider every neighbor, without exception, as another self.

The reality of this human community is as critical to Lili and Jimmy (and as relevant to the issue of the operations they underwent) as it is to those who do not, quite literally, carry their afflictions on their faces. It makes clear our shared obligation to respect the dignity of all human persons—regardless of the burdens with which they were born or which they may acquire later in life. It invites us to consider the place of Jimmy and Lili, and of others like them, in the human community, and to seek the fundamental reason why cosmetic surgery was thought necessary for them.

Lili's and Jimmy's Surgeries Viewed from Medical and Social Perspectives

It is a sad reality that there are those who cannot get past the surface, and who tease and taunt, or perhaps dismiss altogether, those who are not sufficiently fair-of-face to satisfy their high bar of external beauty. Though we may not agree, it is not hard to understand that Jimmy's and Lili's parents sought to erase the triggers of prejudice by

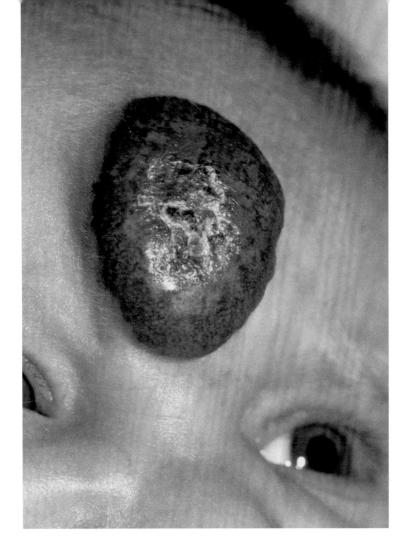

A hemangioma on the forehead of a baby. (Garry Watson/Photo Researchers, Inc.)

"fixing" their faces. Nevertheless, even if, for the sake of argument, we allow them this particular response to the shortcomings of others, ethical questions still remain. Practically, the results of the operations will be different for Lili and Jimmy, and this directs us back to the original question: Are their cases ethically equivalent? To answer that, we must first consider whether they are medically and socially equivalent.

From a medical perspective, both children underwent invasive procedures performed on otherwise healthy bodies. Both operations carried physical risks, none of which was warranted in their cases by medical benefits. Both were performed for the sake of subjectively improving appearance, with the clear hope that that improvement would lead to better social acceptance and personal self-esteem. Both interventions were undertaken by parents who wanted their children to conform to standards of beauty and to an accepted concept of 'normal.' But one critical medical difference does exist: Surgery eradicated a pathology from Lili (the hemangioma), while it only tinkered with the outward signs of Jimmy's (his Down Syndrome). Thus, independent of any other factors (such as comparative risk) the cases are not medically equivalent.

From a social perspective, casual conversations about Jimmy and Lili evoke a gut instinct consensus that there is an essential difference between (a) removing a severely disfiguring (though not life-threatening nor even function-impairing) growth from the face of Lili, and (b) surgically altering Jimmy's Down Syndrome features. There is little doubt that the parents were well intentioned in seeking to remove Lili's hemangioma and to modify Jimmy's distinctive features; little doubt that it was truly the burden of those "scarlet letters" that they sought to remove. In that, their cases are similar.

Yet Lili (like most children who have hemangiomas removed) recovered from surgery with only a faint scar to remind her of the excised growth that had once disgraced her face. Her parents are delighted, and Lili seems pleased. It is hard to imagine a down side to her experience, save for the risk and physical discomfort of the surgery and recovery. Subjectively, it is also hard to imagine that Lili might ever look back and regret that her parents made this choice for her. No studies could be found to rate the reactions of parents and strangers to the esthetic outcome of operations such as hers, but such studies do exist in regard to the surgery Jimmy underwent. A number of those show that while parents (such as Jimmy's) are pleased with the results, independent re-

FAST FACT

According to the National Down Syndrome Society, the life expectancy for people with Down syndrome is fifty-five years.

viewers discern "no improvement in appearance." Other studies dispute the notion that the natural appearance of children with Down Syndrome has any negative effect on how they are perceived. Perhaps they are protected by the features that alert the world that they are coping with the realities of Down Syndrome. Perhaps those features invite understanding and acceptance instead of discrimination. And it is reasonable to surmise that those who would discriminate against Jimmy upon seeing the distinctive features of Down Syndrome, will now discriminate against him once its behavioral and intellectual aspects show themselves. We have to wonder if surgery eliminates or simply delays social disrespect by those so inclined. In any case, the surgical approaches to Lili's and Jimmy's problems are not socially equivalent.

If the studies mentioned above are correct that only parents see significant change, then there is little justification for the risk and suffering of surgery imposed on Jimmy. If, on the other hand, they are wrong, and people do see significant change toward the goal of a 'normal' face, then those other studies that show little correlation between DS features and discrimination remain to argue against surgery. In the light of this conflicting research, and given that surgery does nothing to address the syndrome itself, it is difficult to justify ethically the risks and suffering visited on this child. He remains a person with Down Syndrome, with or without the surgery, and it seems perverse to force him to undergo the pain of surgery in an attempt to accommodate the subjective standards of persons who refused to respect him as he was. According to the principles discussed above, it is those persons who should have accommodated Jimmy, not vice versa.

The Onus to Change Should Be on Society

Lili recovered from surgery looking normal. That is, she looks and behaves like the normal children who are now

The Public Perspectives on the Quality of Life with Down Syndrome

The percentage of responders who believe people with Down syndrome:

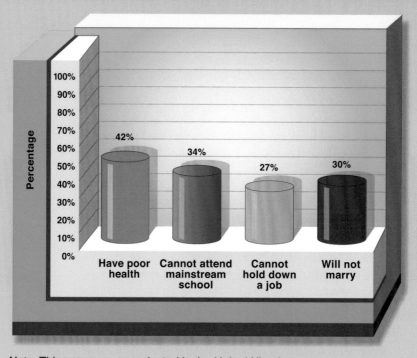

Note: This survey was conducted in the United Kingdom.

Taken from: PR Newswire, "Public Ignorance Is the Biggest Handicap for People with Down's Syndrome, as Survey Shows a 'Reality Gap,'" June 1, 2003.

her full peers (i.e., intellectually, behaviorally, and esthetically), as they would have been from birth if she had never had the hemangioma. The growth thus seems to have been an incidental factor that kept her from assuming her ordered place in society, and with proper care for her well-being, removing it from her was ethically justifiable.

According to his parents, Jimmy recovered from surgery resembling children who do not have Down Syndrome. If they are correct, and the surgery succeeded in its goal, then he no longer resembles the children who had previously constituted his full peer group. Instead, he now looks like children without Down Syndrome, who are neither behaviorally nor intellectually his peers. He has, in effect, been left with no peer group, and will never have one unless (and statistics indicate it is unlikely) a large number of children his age with Down Syndrome undergo the same cosmetic procedures. The surgery has left him a sort of "man without a country." If he is aware of this and is distressed by it, then the surgery is impossible to justify ethically. If he is not aware that he has no full peer group, and is therefore not distressed by that fact, then it is equally difficult to justify the surgical assault on his face. On the other hand, if the independent reviewers are correct that he still looks like a child with Down Syndrome, then the surgery failed in its goal of achieving a normal face for him, and yet again cannot be ethically justified. Whichever scenario exists, and acknowledging his parents' good intentions, one can only conclude that it would have been more ethical to leave his face untouched; to encourage him to grow in self-regard; and to set an example for others in respecting his human dignity. The onus to change should have been on others—not on Jimmy.

Plastic Surgery to Correct Down Syndrome Facial Features Is Ethical

Arthur Caplan

In the following viewpoint, Arthur Caplan addresses North American attitudes toward plastic surgery and specifically, plastic surgery to correct Down syndrome facial features. Caplan argues that the controversy in North America surrounding plastic surgery is a result of our "Puritanical past" and that there is nothing wrong with wanting to look better. He cites evidence that kids, especially teenagers, react negatively to how a child with Down syndrome looks, and asserts there is nothing wrong with electing cosmetic surgery to change the appearance of a child with Down syndrome. Arthur Caplan is director of the Center for Bioethics at the University of Pennsylvania.

When the subject turns to cosmetic surgery, at least among North Americans, two things seem sure to happen—laughter and embarrassment. Laughter because many of the icons of surgical alteration—Michael Jackson, Janet Jackson, Pamela

SOURCE: Arthur Caplan, "You're So Vain—or Maybe Not: What's Wrong with Wanting to Look Better?" *Today,* March 15, 2004. Reproduced by permission of NBC Universal, Inc., All rights reserved.

Anderson—are so distorted as to make us nervous, or their efforts to super-size their body parts seem downright amusing. Embarrassment because so many of us have either thought about undergoing cosmetic surgery or have actually done so.

So is cosmetic surgery simply vain and self-indulgent and therefore immoral? No.

Cosmetic Surgery Is Ethical

American attitudes about cosmetic surgery are very much a product of American culture. Compare U.S. Presidential candidate Sen. John Kerry with Italian Prime Minister Silvio Berlusconi. Kerry has denied rumors that he's used Botox to ease wrinkles on his forehead. Perhaps he fears that such a disclosure—if true—would make him the target of both humor and embarrassment.

As for Berlusconi, he has a lot to be embarrassed about these days but getting a face lift did not faze him in

Many mothers have opted to have their Down syndrome baby's appearance changed with cosmetic surgery so that the syndrome is less noticeable in the child's features. (Markus Dlouhy/Das Photoarchiv/Black Star/Alamy)

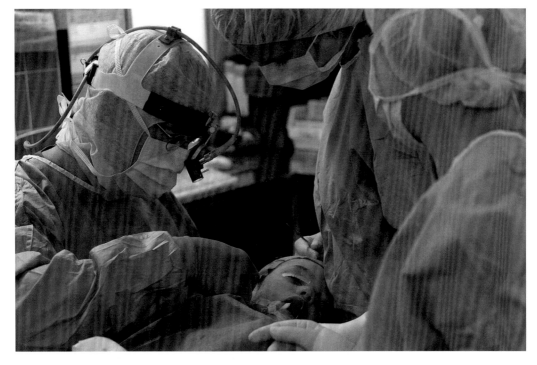

the least. He took a month off to get it done and has been proudly mugging the results ever since.

Even more evidence that our Puritanical past is still alive and well when it comes to surgically tweaking yourself to enhance your looks comes from Brazil. Many Americans who electively undergo the knife deny it. They would no more fess up to a face lift, nose job or liposuction then they would the commission of a major felony. Not so in Brazil. Plastic surgery clinics appear like Starbucks on street corners. If you are wrinkled, unhappy with the size of something or fear some part of you is sagging, the Brazilian attitude is to get it fixed.

Where we see indulgence and vanity, they see only need and reasonableness.

Plastic Surgery and Down Syndrome

All of which brings me to a conversation I recently had with parents whose child has Down syndrome. We all know the classic look of this genetic disorder. My friends worried about other kids reacting negatively to that look and wondered if they should send their child to a plastic surgeon to have his appearance surgically altered.

There is some evidence that kids, especially teen-agers, react negatively to how a child with Down syndrome looks. But there does not seem to be much evidence about how affected kids think about how they look. Surgeons themselves are divided about how well they can alter the appearance of a child with the disorder.

But suppose there is a surgeon who could transform the appearance of a child with Down syndrome to a more "normal" look. Would it be wrong? Some might say it would be fine since a child with the disorder has an abnormal or disfigured face. But is that really the case? Couldn't it be said

---

FAST FACT

According to the American Academy of Pediatrics Committee on Genetics, about 75 percent of children with Down syndrome have some hearing loss, more than 60 percent have vision problems, and 50 percent have heart defects.

Developmental Milestones for Children With and Without Down Syndrome

Milestone	Range for Children with Down Syndrome	Typical Range
Gross Motor		
Sits alone	6 – 30 months	5 – 9 months
Crawls	8 – 22 months	6 – 12 months
Stands	1 – 3.5 years	8 – 17 months
Walks alone	1 – 4 years	9 – 18 months
Language		
First word	1 – 4 years	1 – 3 years
Two-word phrases	2 – 7.5 years	15 – 32 months
Personal/Social		
Responsive smile	1.5 – 5 months	1 – 3 months
Finger feeds	10 – 24 months	7 – 14 months
Drinks from a cup unassisted	12 – 32 months	9 – 17 months
Uses spoon	13 – 39 months	12 – 20 months
Bowel control	2 – 7 years	16 – 42 months
Dresses self unassisted	3.5 – 8.5 years	3.25 – 5 years

Taken from: National Down Syndrome Society, www.ndss.org.

that a kid with Down syndrome has one of a number of looks that human beings are born with?

The decision to try to alter the appearance of a person with Down syndrome would be cosmetic—not reconstructive or therapeutic.

Neither Vain nor Indulgent

I find myself thinking that altering the appearance of a youngster with Down syndrome, if that is what the child and the parents want, would be neither vain nor indulgent. And if that is true then why not admit that Botoxing a wrinkled brow or downsizing a large nose, while cosmetic, may be reasonable choices for some to make as well.

While we love to gossip about and even snigger at those who use cosmetic surgery, maybe we should lighten up a bit. Cosmetic surgery like anything else can be abused or misused, but is it always just unseemly vanity to want to look better?

Assisted Reproductive Technologies Increase the Risk of Birth Defects

Centers for Disease Control and Prevention

In the following press release the Centers for Disease Control and Prevention (CDC) discusses recent CDC-sponsored research that indicates that couples who use assisted reproductive technology (ART) to become pregnant are at a greater risk of birth defects. ART procedures include in vitro fertilization, a process by which egg cells are fertilized by sperm outside the womb, allowed to grow and divide for a few days in a petri dish, and then transplanted into the womb. The researchers examined data from over fourteen thousand births in ten states recorded in the CDC's National Birth Defects Prevention Study. They found that the risk of certain birth defects doubled, and in some cases more than quadrupled, for babies conceived using ART. The CDC is a component of the U.S. Department of Health and Human Services and is the principal U.S. government agency protecting the health and safety of Americans.

SOURCE: Centers for Disease Control and Prevention, "National Birth Defects Prevention Study Shows Assisted Reproductive Technology Is Associated with an Increased Risk of Certain Birth Defects," November 17, 2008. Reproduced by permission.

Infants conceived with Assisted Reproductive Technology (ART) are two to four times more likely to have certain types of birth defects than children conceived naturally, according to a study by the CDC. The report, "Assisted Reproductive Technology and Major Structural Birth Defects, United States," was released in the journal *Human Reproduction*.

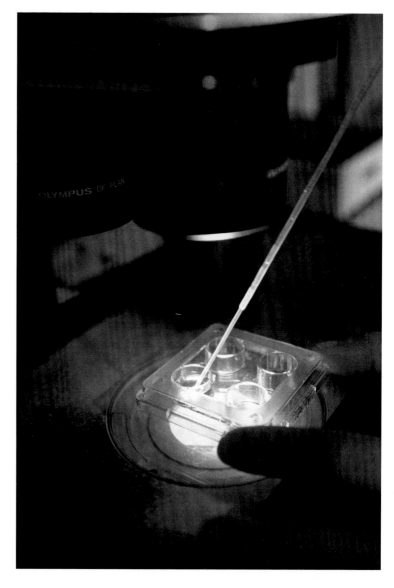

In vitro fertilization is a process by which egg cells are fertilized by sperm outside the womb and allowed to grow in a petri dish. (RAJAU/PHANIE/Photo Researchers, Inc.)

"Today, more than 1 percent of infants are conceived through ART and this number may continue to increase," says Jennita Reefhuis, Ph.D., epidemiologist at CDC's National Center on Birth Defects and Developmental Disabilities. "While the risk is low, it is still important for parents who are considering using ART to think about all of the potential risks and benefits of this technology."

ART Appears to Contribute to the Birth Defect Risk

The study shows that among pregnancies resulting in a single birth, ART (which includes all fertility treatments in which both eggs and sperm are handled, such as in vitro fertilization) was associated with twice the risk of some types of heart defects, more than twice the risk of cleft lip with or without cleft palate and over four times the risk of certain gastrointestinal defects compared with babies conceived without fertility treatments. Despite these findings, the absolute risk of any individual birth defect remains low. In the United States, cleft lip with or without palate affects approximately 1 in every 950 births; doubling the risk among infants conceived by ART would result in approximately 1 in every 425 infants being affected by cleft lip with or without palate.

The study examined multiple births separately from single births because ART increases the chance of a multiple birth. Children born as part of a multiple birth are more likely to have a birth defect regardless of use of ART. The study showed use of ART did not significantly increase the risk of birth defects among multiple births.

However, ART might contribute to the risk of major birth defects by directly increasing the risk of defects among single births. It may also have an indirect impact because ART increases the likelihood of having twins, which is a risk factor for many types of birth defects.

> **FAST FACT**
>
> In 2006, 54,656 infants were born in the United States using assisted reproductive technology.

Researchers believe this suggests the need for further studies to determine risk for ART in pregnancies with multiple births.

The study examined data from 281 births conceived with ART and 14,095 conceived without infertility treat-

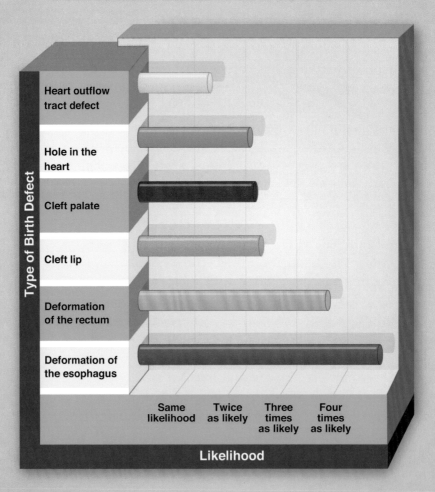

The Increased Risks of Assisted Reproductive Technology

Type of Birth Defect

- Heart outflow tract defect
- Hole in the heart
- Cleft palate
- Cleft lip
- Deformation of the rectum
- Deformation of the esophagus

| Same likelihood | Twice as likely | Three times as likely | Four times as likely |

Likelihood

Taken from: Denise Grady, "Birth Defects Tied to Fertility Techniques," *New York Times*, November 18, 2008. www.nytimes.com.

ments. The National Birth Defects Prevention Study is a population-based study that currently incorporates data from birth defects research centers in Arkansas, California, Georgia, Iowa, Massachusetts, New Jersey, New York, North Carolina, Texas and Utah. These ten centers have been working on the largest study of birth defects causes ever undertaken in the United States. Information is gathered from more than 30,000 participants to look at key questions on potential causes of birth defects. While the causes of most birth defects are unknown, studies show that smoking, alcohol and obesity increase a mother's risk of having a child with a birth defect.

ART Procedures Are Increasing Rapidly

Since 1981, ART has been used in the United States to help women become pregnant. It is defined as any procedure that involves surgically removing eggs from a woman's ovaries, combining them with sperm in the laboratory, and returning them to the woman's body or donating them to another woman. ART does not include treatments in which only sperm are handled (i.e., intrauterine—or artificial—insemination) or procedures in which a woman takes medicine only to stimulate egg production without the intention of having eggs retrieved.

The number of infants born after ART doubled in the United States from 1996 through 2004. According to data from the 2002 National Survey of Family Growth, almost 12 percent of U.S. women aged 15–44 years have reported using infertility services. In 2005, more than 134,000 ART procedures were performed and approximately 52,000 infants were born as a result of these procedures.

The Risk of Birth Defects from Assisted Reproductive Technologies Is Low

Genevra Pittman

In the following viewpoint, Genevra Pittman contends that although Centers for Disease Control and Prevention (CDC) researchers found an increased risk of birth defects for babies conceived using assisted reproductive technology (ART), many issues remain unexplained. Pittman says there is a possibility that the increased risk of birth defects could be caused by underlying health problems in infertile couples, rather than from the ART procedure itself. Additionally, Pittman says that despite the increased risk, the chances of having a baby with a birth defect are still low, even for babies born from in vitro fertilization. Pittman has a bachelor's degree in biology from Swarthmore College and is a contributor to New York University's student-run e-zine *Scienceline*.

A new study supports past findings that children conceived using assisted reproductive technology, such as in vitro fertilization, may be at higher risk for some birth defects than babies conceived naturally. However, speculation remains as to whether the fertility

SOURCE: Genevra Pittman, "Putting a Baby's Risk into Perspective," *Scienceline*, February 2009. Reproduced by permission.

treatments themselves are responsible for the increased risk, or if the reproductive health of patients that turn to these procedures to get pregnant explains the effect.

Researchers Respond to the Study

The recent study, led by Jennita Reefhuis at the Centers for Disease Control and Prevention and published by the journal *Human Reproduction*, identified an increased risk for four of 25 birth defects, including certain heart defects and digestive system abnormalities, for babies born using assisted reproductive technologies. The study data came from a database of nearly 10,000 children born with birth defects and 5,000 healthy children taken from populations of similar parents.

"The study results add further weight to the argument that an increased birth defect risk exists," Michele Hansen, an Australian researcher on assisted reproductive technology, or ART, and child health wrote in an email. "The study adds more information since it is big enough to examine the risk of a number of specific birth defects, which most studies have not been able to do."

Children conceived using ART were about twice as likely to have certain heart defects or to be born with cleft lip and four times as likely to have a defect in the digestive system in which the esophagus or rectum is malformed, compared to those conceived without these procedures. The study found no increase in risk correlated with ART for twins or other multiple births. However, Reefhuis said that this lack of effect may be due to the smaller sample size of multiple births or because children born as part of multiples are known to have a higher risk of birth defects regardless of fertility treatment.

The Underlying Issues with Infertility

In ART procedures, both sperm and eggs are handled outside the body. In vitro fertilization, or IVF, is the most common ART procedure. Sperm and eggs are removed

Conceptions Assisted by Reproductive Technology Pose Some Birthing Concerns

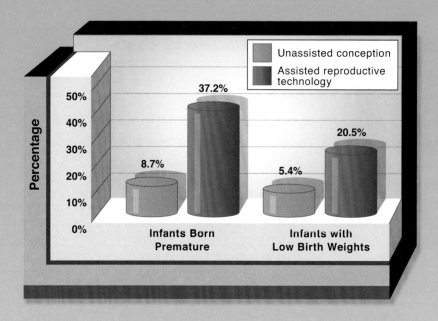

Taken from: J. Reefhuis et al., "Assisted Reproductive Technology and Major Structural Birth Defects in the United States," *Human Reproduction*, vol. 24, 2009.

from the potential mother and father and mixed in a Petri dish. Then the eggs that are successfully fertilized are transplanted back into the uterus. In other ART operations, eggs may be transplanted directly into the fallopian tube. All ART procedures are rare, accounting for only about three percent of infertility services, according to the American Society of Reproductive Medicine. These invasive techniques are generally a last resort for couples trying to have a child when strategies like medication and therapy fail to lead to pregnancy.

"If [the potential parents] are candidates for less aggressive treatments, usually they will do that first," said Dr. Lynn Westphal, head of Stanford University's Fertility and Reproductive Medicine Center. "The people doing IVF are the patients that have no other way to get pregnant."

It is possible that underlying health problems that result in infertility in couples using ART may be accounting for the increased risk of some birth defects in children born using these procedures. "An infertile population is not the same as a regular fertile population," Westphal said. "If you look at couples that have fertility problems, they have [more] problems even if they get pregnant on their own."

Given these underlying issues, some of which may be genetic—abnormalities in a parent's set of chromosomes, where genetic information is located, for example—teasing out which effects are due to the fertility treatments themselves is incredibly difficult. "Ideally we would identify women who have trouble getting pregnant but who do conceive eventually and compare them to women who use ART," Reefhuis explained. She is also planning on looking at women who use fertility drugs to get pregnant, representing a sample that has fertility issues but successfully conceives without undergoing invasive procedures.

Reefhuis hopes that the results of her latest study will help the 7.3 million American women affected by infertility make the decision about how to go forward with fertility treatments. "I really want couples considering ART to be fully informed," she said. "These parents have looked a lot at the risks and benefits. Any additional information is useful."

The Risk Is Small in the End

Both Reefhuis and Hansen emphasized that the increase in risk found in the latest study was a small one and should not necessarily deter couples from using these techniques. "It is important to keep risk estimates in perspective—ART has helped many couples have healthy children, and for those children

> **FAST FACT**
>
> Louise Brown, born in 1978, was the first reported live birth conceived by in vitro fertilization.

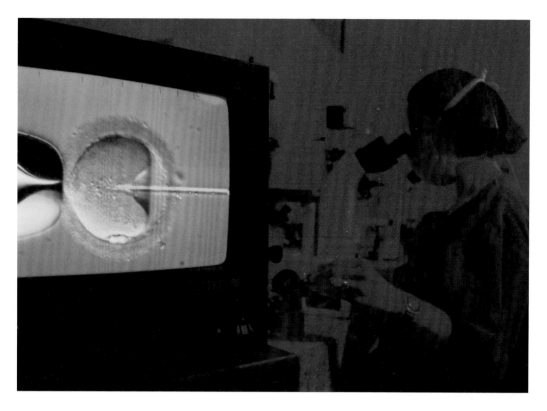

A doctor injects sperm into an egg during in vitro fertilization. (Mauro Fermariello/Photo Researchers, Inc.)

who are affected by a birth defect, many can be treated," Hansen wrote.

Because the chances of having an unhealthy baby are still low, Westphal says the reported increased risk of some birth defects correlated with ART has not been a significant deterrent for the patients she sees. "Usually most of their concerns are about immediate things, concerns about the procedure itself," she said. "I haven't had patients that decided not to [use IVF] because of concerns about increased birth defects. The absolute difference [in risk] is very small. Most children that are born from IVF are normal."

CHAPTER 3

Personal Stories About Birth Defects

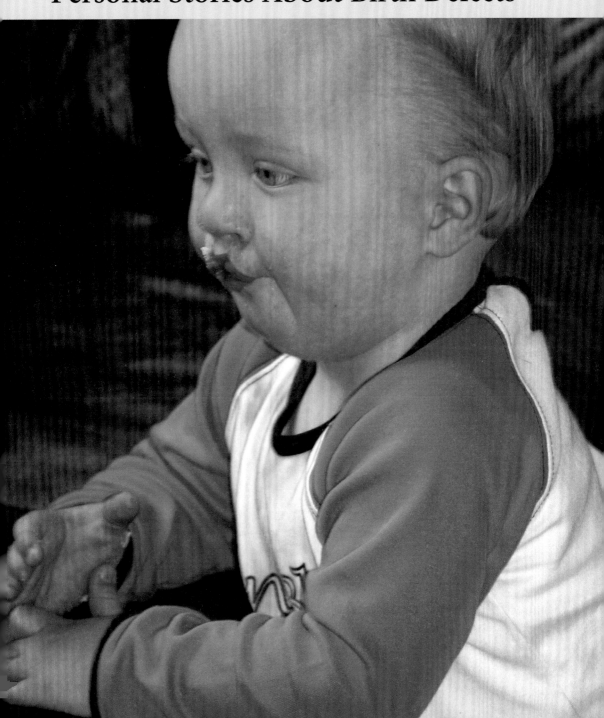

Down Syndrome Does Not Make My Child Defective

Lara Wilkinson

In the following personal story Lara Wilkinson chronicles the life of her young son, Jack, from the moment she learned he had Down syndrome to the celebration of his fourth birthday. Wilkinson describes how at first she was devastated to learn her son had Down syndrome, but she came to accept and embrace his differences. According to Wilkinson, her son has redefined the word perfect: *He has enriched the lives of her entire family and brings joy to all those around him. Wilkinson is a college student, wife, and mother to three young children in Minnesota.*

Every mother dreams of her unborn child and wonders what traits he or she will inherit from the breadth of the family gene pool. Will he have blue eyes like his father? Red hair like his mother? Grandma Nancy's braying laugh or Uncle Robert's tone-deafness? As an expectant young mother, I entertained these kinds

Photo on previous page. A young child with a hairlip may require several corrective surgeries. (Hermien Lam/Catchlight Visual Services/Alamy)

SOURCE: Lara Wilkinson, "The Upside of Down: An Extra Chromosome, an Equal Child," *Exceptional Parent Magazine,* October 30, 2007. Reproduced by permission.

of thoughts, but what my son's genetic legacy entailed—an extra 21st chromosome—I never would have imagined.

My third pregnancy occurred quite unexpectedly, five months after the birth of my second (and I thought, final) child. Overwhelmed at the prospect of having a third child barely a year younger than my middle one, I muddled through the first trimester exhausted, nauseous, and sometimes panic-stricken. Nevertheless, physically, things seemed consistent with my previous pregnancies, and I assumed all was well.

At a doctor's office visit early in my second trimester, I was offered the AFP (Alpha-fetoprotein) screening test. The test, I was told, would measure several substances in my blood. Abnormal levels of these substances could indicate an increased likelihood of certain disorders in a fetus, such as neural tube defects or chromosomal abnormalities. I had declined the test with my previous pregnancies, but this time I felt compelled to rule out any additional surprises; I'd have my hands full enough with a four-year-old, a fourteen-month-old, and a baby. I plopped down in the vinyl-covered lab chair, presented my arm, and with little sense of apprehension, watched the needle draw the blood sample that would shift the course of my life.

Uncertainty Leads to Further Tests

A few days after my appointment, the phone rang. Because I was in the midst of changing my daughter's diaper—an activity in which most of my time seemed to be expended those days—I missed the call. A nurse from the clinic left me a voicemail message indicating little more than that I should call the office when I had a chance. At that moment, I knew something was wrong. I knew that the office might have been calling to request insurance information or to reschedule an appointment, but somehow I sensed otherwise. Unable to reach my doctor for more information, I called my husband. I told him that I believed my AFP had come back with bad results and that the doctor was going to tell me that it indicated an increased likelihood of Down syndrome. At the time, I was only 24 years old and unlikely to have a baby with a chromosomal defect, but I couldn't shake the inexplicable certainty. My doctor called later and confirmed that my fear was not unfounded: the AFP indicated a 1-in-10 likelihood that our baby had trisomy 21, or Down syndrome. She referred me to a specialist for a level-2 ultrasound and further screening.

In the light of the ultrasound screen, I saw images. Some were discernable—a tiny foot, the arc of a round head, a prehistoric-looking spine—but most of it was indistinguishable to my novice eyes. The technician slid the ultrasound wand across my belly, stopping periodically to measure specific parts of the image and enter information on the keyboard of the ultrasound machine. I watched numbers pop on and off in the corner of the screen, and scrambled to make sense of them, hoping to uncover some sign that everything was fine and my baby was perfect. The perinatologist's verdict was that everything looked all right and the gestational dating of my pregnancy was probably off, accounting in part for the abnormal AFP results. I went home hoping that a redraw of the AFP, with current dating, would yield a better result.

A few days after the second AFP screening, I received results indicating the likelihood of Trisomy 21 to be 1 in 21. That was more uncertainty than I could live with for five more months. I had to have an amniocentesis for a definitive answer. We headed back to the perinatologist for the amnio, and awaited results from a preliminary FISH (Fluorescence In Situ Hybridization) test. I had the amnio on a Friday, and we were told to expect the FISH results the following Monday or Tuesday.

Losing the Baby of My Imagination

Monday came, and I was a wreck. I waited anxiously for the phone to ring, desperate to know my baby's fate. The call didn't come. I woke up on Tuesday with a heavy feeling in my stomach. Suddenly, I didn't want the phone to ring. I wanted to believe that the 1-in-21 likelihood was so strongly in our favor that our baby surely didn't have Down syndrome. I felt as though avoiding such an awful truth could prevent it from being so. My doctor called in the evening, and I took the phone into my bedroom and closed the door. "The lab called today with your FISH test results," my doctor said softly, "they told me that your baby does have Down syndrome."

I limped through the conversation, maintaining my composure, as my doctor suggested that my husband and I visit the office to discuss the diagnosis. At the end of the conversation, I hung up the phone and walked into the doorway of the bedroom, looked at my husband, and shook my head. I couldn't speak.

"He doesn't have it?" my husband asked.

"No! He does!" I sputtered. I slammed my fist into the door frame and sank to the floor, sobbing. My husband ushered our two children into one of the other bedrooms, so they could avoid the sight of their mother in tears, crumpled on the carpet. I felt as though I had lost my baby.

In truth, in that moment, I lost the baby I had imagined. My vision of him was inexorably changed, and I no longer knew what to think about him. In fact, I didn't even want to think about him at all.

My Final Months of Anticipation

The subsequent months of my pregnancy were emotionally turbulent. Once we knew that our baby had Down syndrome, our concern shifted primarily to the condition of his heart. The American Academy of Pediatrics states that the incidence of heart defects among children with Down syndrome is about fifty percent. These

> **FAST FACT**
>
> One of the extra 231 genes that Down syndrome people inherit because they have an extra chromosome may inhibit cancer growth, according to a 2009 study reported in the journal *Nature*.

defects can be relatively minor, or they can be fatal. A prenatal echocardiogram done in my 24th week of pregnancy indicated no major defects. At 33 weeks, I had an ultrasound to check for gastrointestinal atresia, another affliction common to children with Trisomy 21, and all appeared well. By all accounts, the major structural issues that were of greatest concern seemed to be nonexistent in our baby. We accumulated a small mountain of black-and-white ultrasound image printouts of our tiny boy, and we decided to name him Jack.

Having accepted the fact that our child would be born with Down syndrome, we grappled with the decision to take the diagnosis as accurate and embrace our child as he would be. Most of our friends and family were supportive of our decision to bring Jack to term, but a few questioned why we wouldn't choose to terminate the pregnancy and absolve ourselves of the responsibility and burden of caring for a child with a disability. More than one well-intentioned person spoke of what they considered to be "God's plan" for Jack, and of the spiritual implications of being "granted" a special child, and "honoring the gift God was giving us." As a lifelong non-religious person, I didn't share their sentiments or believe that some higher power had ordained Jack's disability. To me, my baby was a product of the great diversity of nature. There was no special reason or purpose for his being, and there was nothing inherently wrong about his differences, either. I believed he had the potential to be happy in life—and that, I felt, was what made a life worth living. At my best, I looked forward to the challenge of raising a unique, mold-breaking boy—one whose accomplishments I could relish and whose differences I could celebrate. At my worst, I felt overwhelmed, strangled by my own fear and complete lack of control over the situation, even thinking that it might be best if I simply had a miscarriage. Thirty-seven weeks into the pregnancy, my hopes and misgivings became side notes to the contractions that clutched my abdomen, signaling Jack's intention to join the world outside my body.

I arrived at the hospital 6–7 centimeters dilated and immediately announced that I wanted an epidural. It was my first labor with an epidural, but I was sick, exhausted, and just wanted the pain to stop. The epidural was administered just within the window of opportunity, and by the time it took effect, I was fully dilated. Having never before experienced the luxury of a painless delivery, I rather enjoyed the process, actually laughing when I pushed and felt the baby moving down effortlessly. With little exertion on my part, Jack emerged, tiny and flailing, and the doctor placed him on my chest.

He was small: five pounds, fifteen ounces, and a little over eighteen inches long, but he was healthy. After he was swaddled, I got my first good look at him, and immediately recognized the features characteristic of Down syndrome—the epicanthal folds that cause the appearance of upward-slanting eyes, the squarish head, and the rather flat nose. Foremost, though, he just looked like a newborn baby. He cried, and he sounded like any other baby. He was hungry, and as my other infants had, he rooted for a warm source of nourishment. He was my boy, and all he really needed was me.

Two days later, we returned home from the hospital, and our family flocked to visit us. Everyone wanted to meet our newest little bundle, but he was perpetually asleep—like most newborn babies are.

No Regrets Regarding My Perfect Child

Jack did have a tough time nursing. He had low muscle tone in his mouth, which was very small and filled with a large tongue. We worked with a lactation consultant and were able to use nipple shields to help him latch, and a breast pump to keep my milk supply up. Ultimately, Jack nursed for over a year—longer than my other children had. At his four month check-up, the doctor reviewed his development with me. She laid him on the exam table and asked me if he was rolling over yet. I answered that he wasn't, and Jack proceeded to make a fool of me by promptly rolling over. I laughed, for this was only the first of many times that my boy would prove me wrong when I underestimated him.

When we celebrated his first birthday, Jack wasn't walking yet (most children with Down syndrome aren't at that age), but he was close to crawling. I looked at him as he sat in his high chair, poking at his birthday cake, and for a moment, I wondered what he would've been like on that day if he hadn't been born with an extra chromosome. I imagined the things he would've been doing if he didn't have Down syndrome. Then he looked at me, smiling his trademark gleeful grin, and I knew that there was not a single thing about the way he was that could cause me the slightest regret in making the decision to bring him into our lives. I could never feel sorry about him, especially when he smiled.

He was perfect.

Jack Becomes His Own Person

In the following year, Jack became so adept at crawling that he could virtually run on his hands and knees. Before he turned two, he took his first steps and never looked back. He had physical, occupational, and speech therapists who worked with him regularly, and he had the best teachers of all, his siblings, on duty constantly. His understanding of language was fairly solid, but low oral motor muscle tone made articulating speech difficult for him. Because of this, we used infant sign language with him to help him communicate. Signing allowed Jack to express with his hands what he could not with his voice. His siblings quickly mastered the repertoire of "words" we used and happily participated in signing with Jack as well. Whether at the grocery store, the doctor's office, or in therapy sessions, Jack charmed his victims readily and

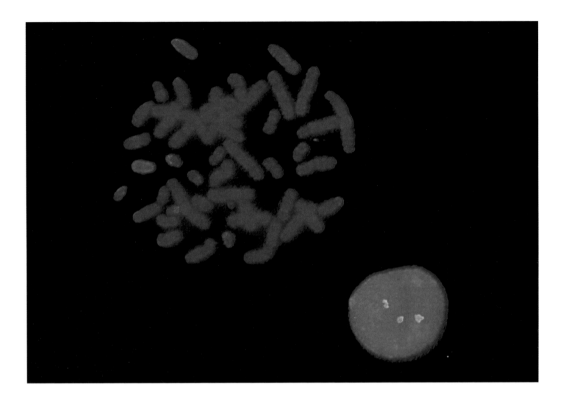

quickly mastered the art of the flirty smile and coyly tilted head. As the months went by, I forgot about the "perfect" child I'd once felt that I "should have had" and came to know the child I had: a perfectly spirited, friendly, motivated, often hilarious little guy.

Several months ago, we celebrated Jack's fourth birthday. He ripped through his gifts with appropriate enthusiasm, and particularly enjoyed his new harmonica, although he was more inclined to lick it than to blow through it. He could barely restrain his excitement at blowing out the candles on his birthday cake. In fact, he feels it to be his duty to help anyone extinguish their candles when he attends a birthday party.

Jack is enrolled in preschool, and on days when school is not in session, he often brings me his backpack and shoes and expresses a desperate desire to go to school anyway. He loves music, has a perfect sense of rhythm,

A FISH micrograph shows chromosomes of a Down syndrome fetus. The pink dots highlight three copies of the Down syndrome chromosome 21. (James King-Holmes/ Photo Researchers, Inc.)

and will dance to anything with a beat. He has the worst excuse for a hairstyle in existence, as he won't hold still long enough for anyone to cut his hair. Sometimes when he's sound asleep, I attempt to trim his disheveled bangs so that his sweet, round eyes will be discernable. He is full of attitude and opinions, and throws passionate tantrums when I hide Mrs. Butterworth, whom he frequently hands me, to indicate that he wants yet *another* Eggo waffle. When I come home from night class at the university, I poke my head in his room and whisper, "I missed you, Jack," and sometimes, if he's still awake, he mumbles back, "I missoo, too."

Diversity as a Teacher

I never envisioned myself raising a child with a disability, but nobody can imagine what it really entails, until they live it. Despite the challenges and the difficulties wrought by having that microscopic extra 21st chromosome, Down syndrome hasn't ruined Jack's life, and it certainly hasn't diminished our family's life together. My older children adore their brother. They show such a profound degree of patience and kindness toward him and each other that I often wonder if I'd ever have been able to instill such qualities in them without Jack's influence. Jack is capable of experiencing and affecting those around him in so many ways that are positive and wonderful that I don't worry much about whether or not he will grow up to live a "good" life; I have little doubt that he will. I believe that the most profound disability in life must be the inability to recognize the value of human diversity. If life is composed solely of what we expect, if all the people we encounter and things we experience conform to some idea of "normalcy," then we're not likely to grow much—as a society, or as individuals.

In the dictionary of my mind, Jack has redefined the word "perfect," and I'm grateful for all that term now means to me.

We Gave Our Baby Back to Heaven

Dayna Olsen-Getty

In the following article, a mother talks about the pain of learning that her unborn child has a severe birth defect. Dayna Olsen-Getty's pregnancy was progressing as normal until, at her twenty-week ultrasound, her baby was diagnosed with acrania (a disorder in which the fetus is missing part or its entire cranium). Olsen-Getty describes her experience with preparing for the short life, and simultaneously, the death of her child.

At my 20-week ultrasound appointment, my husband and I learned that the baby that we are expecting has a fatal birth defect. Sometime very early in his development something went drastically wrong. His skull never formed—the whole top and back part of it simply did not exist. We will probably never find a medical answer to why he developed this way. Babies with acrania have a fairly good chance at living to full term and even some chance of being born alive, but they usually don't live more than a few days after birth. We can expect that if he makes it through birth, our little one will live for just a few minutes or hours.

As Eric and I shared our news about our son's short life expectancy with friends and acquaintances, several people responded by saying that they will be praying for a miracle. We are not particular about who prays for us or how they pray. We are grateful to be upheld in prayer, and we have sensed that we are receiving strength we didn't think we'd have because of these prayers. (Eric commented that he has friends of all three Abrahamic faiths—Christians, Muslims and Jews—praying for our son.) But the choice of some of our friends to pray for a miracle has made me think hard about what I pray for and how I pray.

Preparing for the Baby

When I found out I was pregnant, we were, like most new parents, overjoyed. Once we made it past week 12, when the most serious danger of miscarriage was over, I breathed a huge sigh of relief and settled in to the reality that we were going to have a baby. At his eight-week ultrasound he looked so much like a little sea creature that we started calling him "Flippery." At every checkup, his heartbeat was strong. At 18 weeks, right on schedule, I felt him move. We started collecting donations of baby gear from friends, and I made lists of all the things we still needed to buy. I planned my maternity leave, and we started thinking about how to turn our guest room into a baby room. We signed up for BabyCenter e-mail newsletters, tried out various name possibilities, and even began to think about where our child might go to elementary school. Each week Eric posted updates on Facebook about which fruit or vegetable our little one was currently closest to in size. Eric's mom reported that a flurry of knitting and crocheting was under way in Vermont in preparation for the first grandchild. I compared pregnancy symptoms with my friends who are moms, read pregnancy books, signed us up for birthing classes and started collecting maternity clothes. In every part of our life, we began making room to welcome this little life.

Then came his diagnosis. The very afternoon that we learned of it, we named our son Ethan James. We named him because just an hour before, we had to decide whether we would end his life early or I would continue to carry him until he dies. Eric and I have both spent years as theology students and could easily write papers (and probably a book) about the Christian ethics of this decision, but in the moment there was no need for complex moral reasoning. Only one thing mattered: We love this child. We love him with a love that is far fiercer and stronger than we imagined it could be. All this making room in our lives and getting ready for his arrival had, without our realizing it, made us into parents. We have no power to change anything about his development or diagnosis or the length of his life, but we choose to love him with our whole hearts and to provide for him for as long as God gives him life. We choose to parent him to the best of our ability, even if the time we have with him is achingly short.

FAST FACT

In 2006 about eighteen babies were born with spina bifida—the most common neural tube defect—for every one hundred thousand live births, according to the National Center for Health Statistics.

The Reality of a Short Life

But I am not praying for a miracle. At first, I wondered if this was because I lack faith. It is true that I have a hard time having confidence that God will supernaturally heal those I love when they are deathly ill. Maybe this is because I lived through my mother's excruciating death from cancer, despite many prayers for her healing. Probably it is also because I am culturally a rational Westerner, more likely to put my confidence in the technology of medicine than in the healing power of God.

But the truth is, I saw Ethan's ultrasound photos. I saw with my own eyes that this little boy doesn't have a cranium—the whole top and back of his head are simply missing. On the cross-section scan of his abdomen, I saw the little white oval that is a kidney and the gray empty space on the other side where his second kidney should be, but isn't. We are long past the stage of pregnancy when these structures are supposed to form, and there is no hope that they will spontaneously and naturally form now. I know that it would take a miracle—the ex nihilo, flesh-and-bone-creating kind of miracle—for Ethan to be made whole.

I desperately want Ethan to be born whole. I would give up one of my own arms or legs if it meant that Ethan's skull could close over and his brain form normally. There is nothing I want more in life than to raise this little boy and to have him outlive me. I want to hold his newborn children in my arms when I am old and know that they will live on long after I am gone. But I am not praying for a miracle. I am not capable of praying for healing while simultaneously preparing for Ethan's death. I have to choose one or the other—the two possibilities are simply too much for me to hold together. Eric and I only have this one opportunity, now, in these days of waiting, to parent Ethan well. We don't want to waste this precious opportunity by denying the reality that his life will be very short or by failing to acknowledge that what he needs most from us is our preparation to care for him in his dying.

Parenting While Preparing for Death

Over the past few weeks, Eric and I have begun these strange and unexpected tasks of parenting. With our hospice team, we've started working on a written plan for Ethan's medical care so that he will be protected from pain and surrounded with love as much as possible during the few moments of his life. I have been searching for the right scripture texts and liturgy for his funeral service.

A few nights ago, between work and grocery shopping, we stopped by a baby cemetery. As we walked among the tiny grave plots with their decorations of sippy cups, baby rattles, pinwheels and Matchbox cars, we tried to imagine what it would feel like to bury Ethan there. We have offered his car seat and stroller to friends who are newly expecting and have been shopping instead for a wooden infant casket. Although I haven't found the strength yet to buy anything, I've begun to think about the kind of clothes Ethan will need for his birth and burial. All the while, he kicks away inside of my womb, letting us know that he is still full of life and energy. These are not the tasks I expected to carry out during pregnancy—and they certainly are not on the monthly to-do lists in my pregnancy books—but they are what Ethan needs from us now.

Finding Comfort Through Faith

I have not been praying for the miracle of his healing, but I have been taking great comfort in the miracle that is already assured—the miracle that Ethan's life will not end with his death, but will be joined to the eternal life of the God who made him and gave him to us. Sometimes this promise is offered to people who are grieving as if it is somehow supposed to take away the pain of burying a loved one—and as far as I can tell, it doesn't. My body is still going to ache for him when we come home from the hospital without him. Years from now I will still feel the pain of his absence and wonder about the person he would have grown up to be.

But there is something about his life—the life that God put in him—that is not ephemeral and fragile like his body. In this way, Ethan is no different from any of us. Our bodies are frail and fallible too, and they will all die sooner or later, but we have the promise of resurrection into a life that is not constrained by our frailty and that comes from the One who breathed life into all creation.

A Birth Defect Makes Dating Challenging

Carla Sosenko

In the following article Carla Sosenko describes how she has learned to love herself and accept her birth defect, and she hopes someday to meet a guy who will, too. Sosenko has a rare birth defect that makes her body slightly deformed. Sosenko describes her insecurity at revealing her birth defect to potential suitors. When she finally meets someone who accepts her for who she is, it helps her to accept herself. Sosenko is a writer and editor from New York.

On this first date in a long string of first dates, I'm in a dimly lit bar on New York's Lower East Side, bewitching a stranger with my hip wit, my shiny blonde hair, my ability to keep pace with his drinking. This guy (we'll call him Joel) likes me. I can tell, but then he says so: "This is the best first date I've been on." It's a nice sentiment, but I've heard it before, so I swallow it with a swig of PBR [Pabst Blue Ribbon beer]. It's easy to do when I know he hasn't even seen me yet, not really.

SOURCE: Carla Sosenko, "What the Guys I Date Don't Know," *Marie Claire,* May 2009. Reproduced by permission.

PERSPECTIVES ON DISEASES AND DISORDERS

A Birth Defect Complicates Things

I was born with the rare circulatory disorder Klippel-Trenaunay syndrome (K-T), which translates differently for everyone who has it. For me, it means my right leg is larger than my left and trails slightly when I walk; my back is an uneven, fatty slab with a dense lump above the waist (which a guy in high school once called a meatball); and a gigantic port-wine stain reaches around my broad torso and down toward my right thigh. I know it could have been worse. I might have been blind; I might have needed amputation. I know that I'm lucky.

But K-T definitely complicates things. Tonight Joel hasn't a clue. The dating site where he found me promised that my body type was Average, and as far as he can tell, it is. What else could I have chosen? There was no space for categorizing just my left leg as Slim and my back as Not at All Back-like. No casual way to mention K-T along with my taste for Middle Eastern food and mistrust of cats. I can conceal my body for a time, to a point, with clever dressing and maneuvering, so what Joel sees stacks up to the pictures I've posted: yoga arms, bony clavicle, long, graceful neck in full view. And my pretty face—my beautiful face, if I choose to indulge the flattery I've heard on occasion.

First Dates Are Disposable

He's cute, but nothing terribly special, so when we go on a second date and I struggle to stay awake ("Wow, you play guitar? How fascinating . . . and rare"), it'll be easy to let him go.

I've let a lot of men go, for much lesser reasons than boredom. Tell me you're happy to be out with someone smart and attractive and see if I call you again. E-mail me to say you think I'm pretty—watch what happens. After one date, a med student named Noah IMed to say that my body-type designation of Average was off-base. "You're slender," he said. Noah had seen me in pieces—I'd made sure of it. Then I made sure he wouldn't see me again.

Because they're so disposable, first dates never make me nervous—especially when I stick to my routine. I meet the guy at a bar I've been to so I can take into account the lighting, the dress code, the chairs. Once there, I keep my arms pressed against the drooping jowls of my sides, and my left leg crossed over my right. I flip my hair, display adequate knowledge of indie bands, and thank the bartender each time he refreshes my drink. I think about my sculpted shoulders and that line about how a woman needs a man like a fish needs a bicycle. If my companion suggests something spontaneous mid-date, as a lawyer named Steve once did ("I have an idea—burgers at Shake Shack!"), I'll politely decline and hope he doesn't think I'm difficult. I'll get over it if he does.

But if I make it to a third date, it means I like the guy. That's when I imagine myself as Jaye Davidson in *The Crying Game:* When my secret is revealed—when my date chivalrously ushers me through a door and gets a good look at my back, or kisses me and glides his hand over a ridge he didn't know was there—I am abandoned. Which is why I rarely let things get to that point.

Sometimes, though, my desire to be understood is overwhelming.

An Encouraging Relationship

I met Ross through a mutual friend, but it turns out he'd previously written to me on Nerye.com and been disappointed when I didn't respond. (A little digging through my inbox revealed the reason: He'd specified a weight range in his profile, and even though I fell into it, I'd decided he was shallow.)

The first two dates were uneventful, but we were intrigued enough to keep trying. Our third date was a series of small tragedies. While going through the standard

> **FAST FACT**
>
> The National Organization for Rare Disorders estimates that approximately six thousand rare disorders collectively affect more than 25 million people in the United States.

getting-to-know-you banter, the topic of tattoos came up. Did I have one? I shook my head. "Not even here?" His hand hovered over the small of my back. My heart sank, but I tried to relax.

It was a hot night, so I slipped off my Daryl K zip-up. I had on a short-sleeve Marc by Marc Jacobs top underneath.

"Wow," he said. "Do you work out a lot?"

"Yoga, mostly." I waited a beat before putting my sweatshirt back on in the airless, humid bar.

He stared at me. "Why'd you do that?"

"I'm cold."

"No, you're not," he said. "You didn't like that I noticed your arms."

"It's not my arms," I wanted to say. "It's just, who knows what you'll notice next?" Instead, I changed the subject, and soon we were in the street together, a confusing tension hanging over us. When we passed a psychic shop, I told him I'd always wanted to have my palm read. "Here," he said, grabbing my hands, a flirtatious peace offering. "I'll do it." As he looked at them—not ugly, but large with gaps between the long, skinny fingers, another side effect—he exclaimed with a laugh, "Your hands are so weird!" Before Ross knew what was happening, I had planted a dry peck on his lips and jumped into a cab.

At home I knew the real tragedy had been in not seizing an opportunity. So I sent Ross an e-mail explaining everything. His response was an eloquent missive that built to this: He thought I was beautiful. He'd thought it before and still did.

As we fumbled in our dating over the next few months, our attraction was undone by our preternatural ability to frustrate each other. When we ultimately failed as a couple, it wasn't because of my body. Even our astounding chemistry couldn't make up for the fact that we just couldn't get along.

Which meant a lot, since my body clearly *had* been an issue with other guys, even if we'd never discussed it. Like the one who lent me a pair of shorts to sleep in after a second date and never called again, or the guy I went out with for more than a month who disappeared without warning, then came back a year later seeking friendship. I'd never even had a conversation about my body with

Even as adults, people with birth defects have a difficult time communicating the nature of their handicap to others. (Mikhail Tolstoy/Alamy)

my most serious boyfriend, a wonderful man I dated for a year-and-a-half, not even after his mother grabbed me the first time we met and said cheerfully, "You look different from behind!" Ross was proof that I could reveal myself to someone and he'd still want me.

Loving Myself

My story doesn't begin or end with K-T. I have a full social calendar, a job that I love, excellent clothes, a teeny-tiny nose ring, a filthy mouth, and a badass triangle pose. Most important, I have family and friends who care about me—and if one of them were in my position, I'd tell her that any man who judges her as harshly as she judges herself isn't worth knowing—and I'd mean it. I'd curse a lot and say she doesn't owe anyone an explanation. I'd say, "Repeat after me: 'I'm unique. Got a problem with that? Your loss.'"

So I've updated my dating profile. I don't name my condition, I don't describe it in detail, but there it is, a small, vague shout-out to my uniqueness ("I was born with a bizarro congenital disorder that affects my body a bit") and an invitation to take me or leave me. Now when a guy tries to decide if I'm date-worthy, he can consider the shininess of my hair, the bands I like, and K-T. Because if I can learn to relax a little about it, to love my lumps and bumps, maybe someone else will, too.

Finding Hope Despite a Birth Defect

Ward Foley

In the following excerpt from his second book, Ward Foley talks about growing up with a birth defect called arthrogryposis multiplex congenita, which caused him to have clubbed feet and hands. Foley had loving parents who made him feel normal despite his defect. He loved sports and did not allow his handicap to prevent him from playing ball and riding minibikes. After meeting a young man with the same condition, Foley says he was inspired to write books in order to help others with disabilities and help those without disabilities to understand them. Foley is an author, speaker, husband, and father living in Kansas.

I began my lifelong fight to be "normal" in Sacramento, California, where I was born—with clubfeet and clubbed hands, and without hip sockets and many muscles and tendons. I had struggled to do nearly everything, including staying alive at four months old when I

SOURCE: Ward Foley, *Thank My Lucky Scars: A Memoir*. Norton, KS: ForWard Publishing, 2006. Copyright © 2006 by Ward Foley. All rights reserved. Reproduced by permission.

developed staphylococcus pneumonia. I was saved by a new type of penicillin and the antibiotic chloramphenicol.

My hands were stiffly bent at the wrist and resembled short golf clubs. When I learned to walk at a little over two years old, I did so wearing braces made especially for me. My knees were also stiff and they barely bent, causing me to hobble. This, and my arms swinging back and forth as my body hunched forward, gave my movements a jerky, disconnected appearance.

Wearing braces twenty-four hours a day was very difficult. They were uncomfortable, heavy, and awkward, and their leather straps, tied around my calves, itched constantly. I scratched my legs until they bled.

I hated wearing the braces to bed and learned how to take them off at night and position them perfectly next to my feet under the covers so my parents wouldn't notice I didn't have them on. I thought I was pretty sneaky until years later, when my mom said she had known and had just wanted me to have occasional relief.

At four, I began preschool at Starr King Exceptional, a school for kids with special needs. The next year I was in kindergarten with the so-called normal kids. My teacher was Miss Venables, a former Miss California, and my mom always said she had never before seen so many dads attend parent-teacher conferences. In Miss Venables's class I learned how to tie my own shoes and was rewarded with a sucker, making it an important and memorable day.

Though I struggled throughout my life with trying to be normal, my parents always treated me just like my older brothers, Kirk and Craig, and younger brother, Chris. (Although, when chores needed to be done, I thought they treated me too normally.)

Sports Are a Worthwhile Challenge

I loved sports, and started playing Little League baseball, braces and all, at eight. I was so excited and proud just to be one of the players. I obviously couldn't run as fast, or throw as hard, but I always played my best, and as much as anyone, only later learning the coach had to put each of us in for three innings. But I was really pretty good, batting over .400 throughout my Little League career. Although I looked different from the other kids, baseball made me feel normal and part of a team.

One afternoon, I stood on the sidewalk, watching all my friends play football on neighborhood lawns. (As usual, my brothers wouldn't let me play this rougher game.) The quarterback shouted, "10-24-62-hike," the ball shot back, the pass was in the air, going, going, and then gone . . . right through a neighbor's window. Well, at that point, everyone scattered for cover—except me, stuck not far from the scene of the "crime." I tried to run, but with twenty pounds of braces holding you back, you don't get very far very fast.

The front door opened and the gentleman stood with his hands on his hips. "Who did this?"

I've had many revelations in my life, but few loom as large as this one. No one else would ever be there to answer for me, or take the fall. So I did the only thing a strong, God-fearing youngster could do. I ratted. Yes, I gave every name and where everyone was hiding. As each name was pronounced, the perpetrators slowly emerged from their hiding places and confessed.

My mother and father had taught me about Jesus since the day I was born. Later, whenever I read the "footprints in the sand" poem, about how Jesus carries us in our times of need, I wondered why He didn't carry me a little faster the day the window broke. . . .

Doing Good and Being Bad

At thirteen, I walked twenty miles, and, at fourteen, bicycled forty, and thus raised more than $1,000 for the

March of Dimes. This was money that could help others, but, more important at my age, I won a trip to Disneyland the first year and a minibike the next. People would sponsor my best friend, Andy, at ten cents a mile and me at one dollar. At first I was bothered because they were judging me by the way I looked. Then I realized I would make more. So I happily took their dollars on my way to winning the top prizes.

That minibike was the greatest thing I ever won, but I learned quickly why my parents never wanted me to have a motorcycle.

Within a few weeks, Andy and I had built a wooden ramp in the backyard, found some old milk crates, and began jumping them. I jumped two, three, then four.

"I'm just like Evel Knievel," I said. Andy then suggested I try jumping five.

"I barely made four; five would be crazy."

"C'mon, you can do it. Just take a couple laps in the backyard to build up enough speed."

Reluctantly, I agreed.

Andy rooted me on as I took a few laps and headed for the ramp. "Give it all the gas it's got," Andy yelled.

I turned the throttle as far as I could as I approached the ramp. My hands gripped the handlebars when I hit the air.

"I'm going to make it," I screamed, and I did. Only I forgot to let up on the gas and took off even faster when I again reached the ground.

At full speed I was heading straight toward a wooden fence, twenty feet from where I landed, and my hands were frozen. I crashed through the fence and into the side of the neighbors' aboveground swimming pool. Hundreds of gallons of water poured over me and into our backyard, flowing down onto the patio and almost into our home.

I stood up, soaking wet, a little sore and stiff, with numerous cuts and bruises, but no broken bones. Overall I was fine.

Andy's first words were, "I knew you could make it," and he couldn't stop laughing once he knew I was all right. "Man, you should have seen that."

When I realized I could still walk, I began assessing the situation and just knew my parents were going to kill me. I was scared and already praying when the next-door neighbor walked out back to see his pool flattened and completely emptied, and thirty feet of the fence destroyed.

I begged, "Mr. Kern, please don't tell my parents. I will pay to have this fixed." I only had a couple of dollars; paying for this amount of damage would have taken me years. But I continued to plead with Mr. Kern until he said he would have to think about it for awhile.

One good thing about being disabled is, when I had hurt myself and couldn't walk very well, no one noticed. During dinner that evening, my dad asked my mom if she had seen the backyard. My heart skipped a beat as I continued to chew my food and avoided looking at either of them. "The fence in the backyard is down; it looks like the Kerns' pool broke and our patio is flooded." He continued, "If they think I am paying for part of the fence because of their pool, they're wrong."

Now I was really nervous and tried to finish eating as fast as I could. If my dad knew and was hoping I would say something, I was not. I was taking my chances.

Mr. Kern never said a word to me again about the fence or pool. So many loving and caring people have helped me through life, and he was one example—and not just because he fixed the fence and pool without ever telling my parents.

The Truth About Surgeries and Injuries

Surgeries were difficult, but they become a way of life when you average one nearly every year.

On my tenth birthday, I was in a hospital bed recovering from knee surgery. At 6:00 A.M., I phoned home to

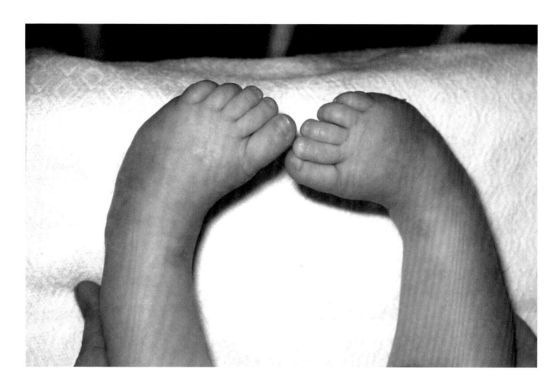

ask Mom when she was coming with my cake and birth-day presents. "I'll be there soon," she promised. Later, I felt bad because, on the way to see me, Mom got a speeding ticket. The officer didn't seem to care she had a lot on her mind and a spoiled, ten-year-old handicapped boy in the hospital, begging her to hurry up.

Ward Foley was born with a birth defect called arthrogryposis multiplex congenita, which includes club-feet. (Dr. M.A. Ansary/ Photo Researchers, Inc.)

Every surgery made me a little better, a little stronger, and life a little easier. My ankles, wrists, and left knee have been reconstructed. I have had pins, screws, and buttons placed in and on my body. I have had bones broken, not by accident, but by my doctors. I have had muscles transplanted and received numerous skin grafts, some of which have actually made for great entertainment. I now have trouble growing hair on my head, but do grow it on the palm of my left hand.

Having had so many surgeries, I felt I had already been through enough for a lifetime and, therefore, more bad things wouldn't happen to me. Yet, I learned early that, just because I had a lot of problems, I wasn't exempt from more.

I worked part-time at a local doughnut shop while attending college. One day, five minutes before my shift ended, I slipped and fell. Both hands, up to my wrists, went into the 400-degree fryer.

My doctor impressed upon my mother and me the importance of keeping my hands clean. The first time Mom poured water on the tissue of my burned hands, I screamed in agony. Never getting upset, she stayed calm, continued washing my hands, and tried to help me relax. These burns provided some of the worst pain I have ever experienced. I now have an understanding of, and great empathy for, burn victims. . . .

Surgeries Were Only Part of a Solution

Years earlier, doctors had taken my pectoral muscles and built me biceps. The rehabilitation was quite interesting since my mind still thought those muscles were in my chest. Thus, in the early days, I had to think one direction in order to make my arms move another.

For example, in order to bring my arm down when it was straight out to my side, I would mentally have to pull it downward, since its natural behavior was for my elbow to bend with my hand coming toward my face. This was bizarre, but the exercises went well, until the day came when I was struggling to pull my arm down and, suddenly, my hand smacked me in the face.

Still, before the surgery, I could barely lift a glass of water with both hands. Now I can lift several pounds with one arm.

I had dealt with all the surgeries very well. Seeing progress, realizing that each operation enabled me to look better and do more, helped me accept all the pain. Being teased, made fun of, and laughed at was more difficult. Feeling less a person because of others—and myself—was also very hard.

When I looked in the mirror, I had to like what I saw before anyone else would. Accepting my abilities and disabilities with a positive attitude was one of the hardest challenges I faced. A friend once told me that God does not give us a good life or a bad life; rather, happiness is a choice. God gives us life, and we make it good or bad. I was also taught by my parents to look for the good in things and focus on what I *can* do.

All this is much easier said than done.

Seeing Myself Through Others' Eyes

When I was nineteen, my doctor gave my phone number to a couple whose son was born with the same condition I had—Arthrogryposis Multiplex Congenita (AMC). They called, believing it would help Paul to talk to someone who had experienced and survived what he was going through. I agreed, and was actually excited because I had never before met anyone with the same condition.

Thirteen-year-old Paul came into the room, and I was struck by how different we looked. I thought, "Oh, he is so much worse than I am and obviously hasn't had the great doctors I have had."

Paul was a very nice young man, and we talked with my and his parents for awhile, and then he and I went out and talked some more. I felt sad for him, because I, in a sense, could feel his pain. Not his physical pain, but the years of emotional tension to come. It seemed to me the hardest years were between thirteen and the early twenties, and I was emerging from them. He was only beginning down the path. The difficulties with relationships, like girls who said they really liked me but only wanted to be my friend, and the emotional ups and downs every teenager experiences—compounded by the physical deformities that set us apart from others—would only worsen for him, while for me, they were subsiding.

I knew what he had to look forward to during high school and I was glad that, when he saw me, he saw someone who had "made it through." I hoped that helped him. I know Paul and his parents thanked us profusely for the chance to talk and find hope.

For all the help they seemed to feel I had given Paul, he gave me much more. I actually felt blessed in not looking much like him and being so much better off.

After they were gone my mother said, "Ward, he looks just like you. Isn't that amazing?"

"I don't look at all like that," I replied, a bit indignant.

"You are mirror images of each other," said my father.

This was the first time I had a glimpse of myself through others' eyes, and I was shocked and upset. I didn't like what I saw, especially the way I looked on the inside. For I realized that, no matter how much I had tried to convince myself I was normal, I didn't believe it. On the outside I may have appeared to be at peace with myself, but, on the inside, I wasn't.

However, while trying to help Paul, I also discovered a need to help others. Not until much later would I realize how this desire to help others was going to help me.

The First Book

Immediately after meeting Paul, I decided to write a book. It took me many attempts, but finally I completed *God Didn't Make Me a Woman Because I Had Enough Problems*. When my mother asked about the title, I explained, "Mom, you and Grandma both worked full-time jobs and took care of the family, and I couldn't have done it all." Although I chose the title because I thought it was catchy and funny, I truly believed what I told my mother.

That book was both an endeavor to help others and to explore my own feelings about my life, but I knew I wasn't the greatest writer. In fact, I had to agree with most of a newspaper book reviewer's less-than-positive assessment. However, I felt he had missed the point when he said my writing skills were as clumsy as the way I walked!

Funny thing though. That didn't upset me; instead, it only reinforced my belief that what I was doing—trying to help people understand handicaps—was important. With that purpose and that accomplishment, I finally felt I was heading in the right direction.

GLOSSARY

Accutane A prescription medication used to treat acne that can cause miscarriage or birth defects when taken during pregnancy.

achondroplasia A common group of growth defects characterized by abnormal body proportions. Affected individuals have arms and legs that are very short, while the torso is nearly normal size.

agenesis The failure of an organ to develop during embryonic growth and development.

alpha-fetoprotein (AFP) A protein produced by a growing fetus; it is present in amniotic fluid and, in smaller amounts, in the mother's blood.

amniocentesis A prenatal test that involves inserting a needle through the mother's abdominal and uterine walls and into the amniotic sac to retrieve a small sample of amniotic fluid and analyze it to determine chromosomal and genetic disorders of the developing fetus.

amniotic fluid A clear, yellow-colored fluid that surrounds the fetus in the uterus, helps protect the fetus from injury, and regulates the temperature of the fetus.

anencephaly A type of neural tube defect that occurs when the fetus's head and brain do not develop normally. Babies with anencephaly are either stillborn or die shortly after birth.

antenatal Refers to the prenatal period; before birth.

arthrogryposis A congenital disorder marked by generalized stiffness of the joints, often accompanied by muscle and nerve degeneration, resulting in severely impaired mobility of the limbs.

atresia A congenital absence or closure of a normal body opening (anus) or tubular structure (esophagus or intestines).

atrial septal defect (ASD)	A congenital heart defect characterized by one or more openings in the atrial septum, which is the wall between the right and left atria.
birth defect	An abnormality of structure, function, or metabolism (body chemistry) present at birth that results in physical or mental disabilities or death.
cerebral palsy	A group of conditions that affect movement, balance, and posture. Affected children have abnormalities in one or more parts of the brain that affect the ability to control muscles.
chorionic villus sampling (CVS)	A prenatal procedure involving the removal of a small amount of placental tissue and its analysis for certain genetic abnormalities and chromosomal disorders.
chromosomes	Structures in cells that carry genes and are made up of DNA. Humans have twenty-three pairs of chromosomes; one member of each pair is inherited from the mother, the other from the father. Each chromosome can contain hundreds or thousands of individual genes.
cleft lip/cleft palate	One of the most common birth defects. It is caused by abnormal facial development that creates a cleft or opening in the lip (cleft lip) or the hard or soft palate of the mouth (cleft palate). Cleft lip and palate can occur together or alone.
clubfoot	Any number of foot abnormalities present at birth. The defect can be mild or severe, and it can involve one or both feet. The medical term for clubfoot is *talipes equinovarus*.
congenital	Refers to being present at birth.
congenital heart disease/defect	A structural or functional heart problem present at birth.
cystic fibrosis (CF)	An inherited disease that affects the lungs and digestive system.
Down syndrome (trisomy 21)	A chromosomal abnormality characterized by an extra copy of chromosome 21. Down syndrome is characterized by moderate to severe mental retardation, a sloping forehead, small ear canals, a flat-bridged nose, and short fingers and toes.

Edwards syndrome (trisomy 18)	A chromosomal abnormality characterized by an extra copy of chromosome 18. Edwards syndrome is characterized by mental retardation, neonatal hepatitis, low-set ears, skull malformation, and short digits. Cardiac and renal anomalies are also common. Most infants with Edwards syndrome die after only a few months.
encephalocele	A protrusion of the brain through a defect in the skull.
fetal alcohol syndrome (FAS)	A collection of growth, mental, and physical problems that may occur in a baby when a mother drinks alcohol during pregnancy.
fetus	An unborn baby from the eighth week after fertilization until delivery.
folic acid	A type of B vitamin that can help prevent birth defects of the brain and spinal cord called neural tube defects (NTDs). Folic acid works to prevent these birth defects only if taken before conception and during early pregnancy.
fragile X syndrome	An inherited form of mental retardation.
gastroschisis	A defect in the fetal abdominal wall in which the bowel protrudes through the opening and floats freely in the amniotic fluid.
genes	DNA "blueprints" that code for specific traits, such as hair and eye color.
gestation	The length of a pregnancy; the number of weeks from conception until birth.
hydrocephalus	A buildup of cerebrospinal fluid that may cause the pressure inside the head to increase and the skull bones to expand to a larger-than-normal appearance.
intracytoplasmic sperm injection (ICSI)	An in vitro fertilization procedure in which a single sperm is injected directly into an egg.

in vitro fertilization (IVF)	A treatment for infertility whereby a woman's egg cells are fertilized by sperm outside the womb, i.e., in a petri dish, and then transferred back into the woman.
level II ultrasound	A detailed, or "targeted," ultrasound, in which ultrasound experts identify and assess fetal abnormalities.
low birth weight	A birth weight of less than 5 pounds, 8 ounces (2,500g), according to the March of Dimes. Low-birth-weight babies are at increased risk for serious health problems as newborns, lasting disabilities, and even death.
lower limb deficiencies	The absence of a portion of the lower limb.
Marfan syndrome	A genetic disorder that affects connective tissue.
microcephalus	An abnormally small head and underdeveloped brain.
neonatal intensive care unit (NICU)	A special-care nursery that uses advanced technology and trained health professionals to care for sick and premature newborns.
neural tube defect (NTD)	Birth defects of the brain and spinal cord. These defects occur around the twenty-eighth day after fertilization and result when the neural tube—the precursor to the spine and brain in the developing fetus—fails to close properly. The two most common neural tube defects are spina bifida and anencephaly.
open fetal surgery	A surgery performed on a fetus still inside the mother's womb.
placenta	An organ that only grows in the uterus during pregnancy and provides nourishment to and takes waste away from the fetus.
premature	Babies born before thirty-seven completed weeks of pregnancy.
prenatal	Refers to the period before birth.
sickle-cell anemia	An inherited disease of red blood cells. Individuals with sickle-cell disease have abnormal hemoglobin, the protein inside red blood cells that carries oxygen to every part of the body.

spina bifida	A neural tube defect that results from incomplete closure of the fetal spine. There is usually nerve damage that causes at least some paralysis of the legs.
Tay-Sachs disease	An inherited disease of the central nervous system caused by a defect in a single gene. Tay-Sachs disease causes deterioration of mental and physical abilities that commences at six months of age and results ultimately in death, usually by the age of four.
teratogen	Any substance or agent that can alter development and result in a birth defect.
teratology	The study of teratogen-caused birth defects.
thalidomide	A drug used to treat many common ailments, including morning sickness in pregnant women, in the late 1950s and early 1960s. It was widely used in many countries but was never approved for use in the United States. It was found to cause serious birth defects.
trimester	A time period of approximately three months, or one-third of a pregnancy.
ultrasound	A diagnostic imaging technique that uses high-frequency sound waves and a computer to create images of blood vessels, tissues, and organs. In pregnancy the sound waves create an image of the fetus's body and organs, as well as surrounding tissues.
upper limb deficiencies	The absence of a portion of the upper limb.
uterus	A hollow, pear-shaped organ located in a woman's lower abdomen, between the bladder and the rectum, that sheds its lining each month during menstruation and in which a fertilized egg (ovum) becomes implanted and the fetus develops.
ventral wall defect	A congenital abnormality in the abdominal wall that allows organs to protrude through the abdominal wall.

CHRONOLOGY

ca. 1500 B.C.	Biblical passages refer to the teratogenic effects of alcohol.
ca. 670–625 B.C.	The Tablet of Nineveh, written by the Chaldeans, is reported to be the first written record of teratology and malformations. It contains a list of sixty-two malformations, including the interpretation of the birth defects. These malformations were used to predict the future; for instance, if a child is born without a right hand, the country will be convulsed by an earthquake.
ca. 400–325 B.C.	Aristotle and Hippocrates believe that mechanical forces such as uterine pressure or trauma can induce birth defects.
ca. 400 B.C. to the late 1800s	It is thought that the embryonic formation of a child is influenced by *maternal impressions* such as the thoughts, emotions, and perceptions of the pregnant mother; for instance, if a pregnant mother views someone with a shocking deformity, her baby will be deformed.
ca. 1400–1500	Children born with malformations such as clubfoot are believed to be offspring of the devil. These children and/or mothers are often put to death.
1573	Ambroise Paré, in his book *On Monsters and Marvels*, lists thirteen possible causes of birth defects, such as the glory or wrath of God, a narrow or small womb, the posture of the mother, heredity or accidental illness, or "rotten seed."

1651   William Harvey proposes the theory of arrested development as a cause for malformation.

1772–1844   Étienne Geoffroy de Saint-Hilaire demonstrates through comparative anatomy that a cause of "monstrosity" is an interruption in the development of the fetus.

1866   British doctor John Langdon Down describes Down syndrome.

1891   Camille Dareste writes *On Monsters and Causalities in Teratology* and determines that different teratogenic agents will result in similar developmental alterations through developmental arrest.

1897   Austrian doctor Victor Eisenmenger describes a type of congenital heart disease in which a hole exists between the heart's two chambers.

1900   One-quarter of all American babies die before they reach age five.

1902–1904   J.W. Ballantyne writes a two-volume text titled *Manual of Antenatal Pathology and Hygiene,* which discusses the anatomy and physiology of the fetus, as well as the social impact of human malformations. Ballantyne stresses that the cause of birth defects should be a physician's primary focus, because this knowledge will aid in the prevention of future malformations.

1908   English physician Archibald Garrod presents the concept of inborn errors of metabolism.

1922   Julius Hess publishes *Premature and Congenitally Diseased Infants.*

1936   Maude Abbott publishes the *Atlas of Congenital Heart Disease.*

1939   The first March of Dimes chapter is established in Coshocton, Ohio; the first successful repair of esophageal atresia is performed.

1941   Sir Norman McAllister Gregg recognizes that fetuses exposed to the rubella virus *in utero* have increased eye, heart, and ear defects as well as decreased IQ and speech impediments.

1945   Clement Smith publishes *The Physiology of the Newborn Infant.*

1950s   Scientists first suggest a link between neural tube birth defects such as spina bifida and diet.

1952   Virginia Apgar develops the Apgar score, a clinical system for evaluating an infant's physical condition at birth; English physician Douglas Bevis publishes an article in the journal *Lancet* describing his use of amniocentesis to identify risk factors in the fetuses of Rh-negative women.

1956   Albert Levan and Joe Hin Tjio discover that the correct number of human chromosomes is forty-six; F. Fuchs and P. Riis are the first to use amniotic fluid to identify genetic disease and congenital abnormalities.

1959   Jérôme Lejeune links trisomy 21 to Down syndrome; James Wilson introduces the six principles of teratology, which are still applied today, in his monograph *Environment and Birth Defects.*

Late 1950s and early 1960s	More than ten thousand children in forty-six countries are born with deformities after their mothers took thalidomide to relieve morning sickness.
1961	Thalidomide is withdrawn from the market worldwide. It was never approved in the United States, and only seventeen American babies are affected.
1968	Carlo Valenti is the first to diagnose Down syndrome using amniocentesis; Jan Mohr introduces the concept of prenatal genetic testing using chorionic villi, and then with N. Hahnemann develops the chorionic villus sampling technique.
1973	David Smith, Ken Jones, and others coin the term "fetal alcohol syndrome" to describe a pattern of birth defects found in children of mothers who consumed alcohol during pregnancy.
1973	April Murphy is the first baby to be treated successfully in the womb for birth defects.
1982	Baby Doe is born with severe birth defects in Bloomington, Indiana. He dies one week later amid controversy over his parents' decision to forgo a surgery that could have prolonged his life, though it would not have corrected all of his birth defects.
1984	The Baby Doe amendment to the Child Abuse Law is enacted.
1992	The U.S. Food and Drug Administration recommends fortifying the nation's food supply with folic acid to reduce birth defects.

1998   The United States and Canada begin requiring that folic acid be added to flour, breads, and other grain products; Congress passes the Birth Defects Prevention Act of 1998.

2007   The American College of Obstetricians and Gynecologists recommends that all pregnant women, regardless of their age, should be offered screening for Down syndrome.

ORGANIZATIONS TO CONTACT

The editors have compiled the following list of organizations concerned with the issues debated in this book. The descriptions are derived from materials provided by the organizations. All have publications or information available for interested readers. The list was compiled on the date of publication of the present volume; the information provided here may change. Be aware that many organizations take several weeks or longer to respond to inquiries, so allow as much time as possible.

American College of Obstetricians and Gynecologists (ACOG)
409 Twelfth St. SW
PO Box 96920,
Washington, DC
20090-6920
(202) 638-5577

The ACOG is a nonprofit organization of professionals providing health care for women. The ACOG advocates for quality health care for women, promotes patient education, and increases awareness among its members and the public of the changing issues facing women's health care. The ACOG issues important guidelines and bulletins and publishes several journals such as *Obstetrics & Gynecology* and *Special Issues in Women's Health.*

Birth Defect Research for Children (BDRC)
800 Celebration Ave.,
Ste. 225, Celebration,
FL 34747
(407) 566-8304
fax: (407) 566-8341
www.birthdefects.org

The BDRC is a nonprofit organization that provides parents and expectant parents with information about birth defects and support services for their children. The BDRC has a parent-matching program that links families who have children with similar birth defects. The BDRC also sponsors the National Birth Defect Registry, a research project that studies associations between birth defects and exposures to radiation, medication, alcohol, smoking, chemicals, pesticides, lead, mercury, dioxin, and other environmental toxins.

Centers for Disease Control and Prevention (CDC) National Center on Birth Defects and Developmental Disabilities/Division of Birth Defects and Developmental Disabilities
1600 Clifton Rd., MS E-86, Atlanta, GA 30333
(800) 232-4636
www.cdc.gov/ncbddd/index.html

The CDC is a component of the U.S. Department of Health and Human Services. The CDC is the nation's premier health promotion, prevention, and preparedness agency. The National Center on Birth Defects and Developmental Disabilities (NCBDDD) is dedicated to helping people with birth defects and disabilities live to the fullest. The CDC and the NCBDDD monitor birth defects prevalence, work to prevent birth defects, conduct birth defects research, and fund the birth defects research of others. The CDC and the NCBDDD publish numerous brochures, booklets, and fact sheets on specific birth defects, birth defects statistics, and birth defects prevention.

Federation of American Societies for Experimental Biology (FASEB)
9650 Rockville Pike, Bethesda, MD 20814
(301) 634-7000
fax: (301) 634-7001

The FASEB is a coalition of independent member societies such as the American Society for Nutrition and the Endocrine Society that serve the interests of biomedical and life scientists. The FASEB advances health and welfare by promoting progress and education in biological and biomedical sciences through service to its member societies and collaborative advocacy. The federation publishes the *FASEB Journal* each month.

March of Dimes Birth Defects Foundation
1275 Mamaroneck Ave., White Plains, NY 10605
(914) 428-7100
fax: (914) 428-8203
www.marchofdimes.com

The March of Dimes is one of the oldest U.S. organizations devoted to improving the health of babies. The March of Dimes raises money to help prevent birth defects, genetic disorders, premature births, and infant deaths. The March of Dimes carries out its mission through research, community service, education, and advocacy. The organization publishes a monthly e-mail newsletter called *Miracles*.

National Down Syndrome Society (NDSS)
666 Broadway, 8th Fl.,
New York, NY 10012
(800) 221-4602
www.ndss.org

The NDSS envisions a world in which all people with Down syndrome have the opportunity to enhance their quality of life, realize their life aspirations, and become valued members of welcoming communities. The mission of the NDSS is to be the national advocate for the value, acceptance, and inclusion of people with Down syndrome. The organization advocates for improved public policy, increased public resources, and services for people with Down syndrome. The NDSS publishes an annual newsletter.

National Organization for Rare Disorders (NORD)
55 Kenosia Ave., PO Box 1968, Danbury, CT 06813-1968
(203) 744-0100
fax: (203) 798-2291
www.rarediseases.org

NORD is a nonprofit organization composed of voluntary health organizations dedicated to helping people with rare diseases and assisting the organizations that serve them. NORD is committed to the identification, treatment, and cure of rare disorders through programs of education, advocacy, research, and service. The organization publishes books and guides such as the *NORD Resource Guide*, where families can find sources of help and encouragement, and the *NORD Guide to Rare Disorders*, a textbook for physicians and health-care providers. The *Orphan Disease Update* is a newsletter published by NORD three times per year.

National Society of Genetics Counselors
233 Canterbury Dr.,
Wallingford, PA 19086-76708
(610) 872-7608
www.nsgc.org

The mission of the National Society of Genetic Counselors is to advance the various roles of genetic counselors in health care by fostering education, research, and public policy to ensure the availability of quality genetic services. The society promotes the professional interests of genetic counselors and provides a network for professional communications. The society's publications include *Perspectives in Genetic Counseling* and the *Journal of Genetic Counseling*.

**Spina Bifida
Association (SBA)**
4590 MacArthur
Blvd. NW, Ste. 250,
Washington, DC
20007
(202) 944-3285
fax: (202) 944-3295
www.spinabifida.org

The SBA serves adults and children who live with the challenges of spina bifida. The SBA is a national voluntary health agency dedicated to enhancing the lives of those with spina bifida and those whose lives are touched by this challenging birth defect. Its tools are education, advocacy, research, and service. The SBA publishes a quarterly magazine called *Insights into Spina Bifida.*

Teratology Society
1821 Michael Faraday
Dr., Ste. 300, Reston,
VA 20190
(703) 438-3104
fax: (703) 438-3113
http://teratology.org

The Teratology Society was formed in 1960 to foster the exchange of information relating to congenital (birth) defects, including their nature, cause, mechanism, and prevention. *Birth Defects Research* (formerly known as *Teratology*) is the official journal of the society. It is a three-part journal that publishes animal, clinical, and experimental research papers, as well as reviews and other pertinent material relating to congenital malformations.

FOR FURTHER READING

Books

Daphne Blunt Bugental, *Thriving in the Face of Childhood Adversity.* New York: Psychology Press, 2003.

Arthur Caplan, Robert Blank, and Janna Merrick, eds., *Compelled Compassion: Government Intervention in the Treatment of Critically Ill Newborns.* New York: Humana, 1992.

Janny Dicken, *Cody's Story: Living One Day at a Time with Spina Bifida.* Baltimore, MD: Publish America, 2005.

Janet V. Engels, *Birth Defects: New Research.* Hauppauge NY: Nova, 2006.

Jonathan Glover, *Choosing Children: Genes, Disability, and Design.* New York: Oxford University Press, 2006.

Ruth Levy Guyer, *Baby at Risk: The Uncertain Legacies of Medical Miracles for Babies, Families, and Society.* Sterling, VA: Capital, 2006.

Patrick Henry Hughes, Patrick John Hughes, and Bryant Stamford, *I Am Potential: Eight Lessons on Living, Loving, and Reaching Your Dreams.* Jackson, TN: Da Capo, 2008.

Phillip Knightley, *Suffer the Children: The Story of Thalidomide.* Glasgow: Andre Deutsch, 1979.

Bryan Lambke and Tom Lambke, *I Just Am: A Story of Down Syndrome Awareness and Tolerance.* Chandler, AZ: Five Star, 2006.

Tracie Martin, *Interests in Abortion: A New Perspective on Foetal Potential and the Abortion Debate.* Surrey, UK: Ashgate, 2000.

Keith Moore, T.V.N. Persaud, and Mark Torchia, *Before We Are Born: Essentials of Embryology and Birth Defects.* Amsterdam: Saunders/Elsevier, 2008.

Allen Shuh, *The Story of Bella.* Canton, MI: Zoe Life, 2007.

Peter Tallack, *In the Womb.* Washington, DC: National Geographic Society, 2006.

Marelyn Wintour and Julie Owens, *Early Life Origins of Health and Disease.* Boston: Birkhäuser, 2006.

Mitchell Zuckoff, *Choosing Naia: A Family's Journey*. Boston: Beacon, 2002.

Periodicals

Joseph Berger, "Beauty in a Parent's Eyes, and in the Face of a Child," *New York Times*, June 15, 2008.

C. Brownlee, "Bridging the Divide? Technique Sheds Light on Cleft Palate Gene," *Science News*, February 17, 2007.

C. Dyer, "Judge Rules That Birth Defects Could Have Been Caused by Toxic Waste from Steel Works," *British Medical Journal*, 2009.

Exceptional Parent, "Spina Bifida and Folic Acid Awareness," December, 2007.

Carey Goldberg, "New Birth Defect Treatment Studied," *Boston Globe*, May 14, 2006.

GP, "Behind the Headlines: Is Chlorine in Tap Water Linked to Birth Defects?" June 13, 2008.

Harvard Reviews of Health News, "Birth-Defect Rate Triple for Diabetic Moms," July 31, 2008.

Nicholas Kristof, "It's Time to Learn from Frogs," *New York Times*, June 28, 2009.

Jessica Long, "I've Never Really Felt My Disability," *Shape*, August, 2008.

Henry Schulman, "Good Bet Against Long Odds; New Giant Left His Birth Defects in the Dust," *San Francisco Chronicle*, August 7, 2009.

Andrea Stone, "The Day I Considered Abortion: Could I Trust God Despite My Baby's Potential Birth Defects?" *Today's Christian Woman*, March–April 2008.

Toronto Star, "Doctors Under Scrutiny over Duty of Care to Unborn," August 31, 2009.

P. Wentzel, "Can We Prevent Birth Defects with Micronutrients?" *Diabetes, Obesity & Metabolism*, August 2009.

Michael Winerip, "Taking a Chance on a Second Child," *New York Times*, May 11, 2008.

Women's Health Weekly, "Immigrant Women May Be at Higher Risk of Having a Baby with a Birth Defect," April 30, 2009.

INDEX